The Garden Art of China

Si Yuan (West Garden) of Yi Miao (City Temple), the predecessor of Yu Yuan, Shanghai, mid-18th century.

中國造園藝術
The Garden Art of China

by

Chen Lifang and Yu Sianglin

TIMBER PRESS
Portland, Oregon

© Timber Press 1986

All rights reserved.
Printed in Hong Kong
Book design: Sandra Mattielli

ISBN 0-88192-002-9

TIMBER PRESS
9999 SW Wilshire
Portland, Oregon 97225 USA

Contents

1   Introduction

China's classical artistic sensibilities and works have been well known worldwide for some centuries. Her tradition of landscaping art has influenced garden design widely, first in Japan and then, by the latter part of the 18th century, Europe.

Historically, Chinese landscape architecture can be classified into two general patterns: the first was the imperial palace garden complexes, such as the Summer Palace outside Peking; the second, and more common, were the private, residential gardens located in cities. The imperial gardens were sited in naturally scenic rural locations and constructed on a large scale together with magnificent buildings to house the court. Great ingenuity was required to build the smaller residential gardens in cities. Within the limited space available the typical residential garden was laid to conform to the artistic conventions of landscape painting. Its internal structure was based on natural landscapes and the skills of traditional architects in keeping with the five elements of horticultural design: traditional Chinese style architecture, rock gardens, waterscapes, flowers and trees.

Rock gardens were built up to create changing perpendicular lines in space and to make divisions between garden scenes often used to support a planting of vines. Waterscapes were used both to create and delineate a natural scene and to give a perception of a larger space in a small area. Flowers and trees were used in conventional ways depending upon climate, scenic requirements and the personal preferences of the owner. The gardens of Soochow typify this traditional approach to residential garden design.

The residential gardens of Soochow had as their focus the residence which was surrounded by a series of connected gardens and courtyards designed to reproduce a variety of natural scenes. Through the skillfull use of shade, layers of plants, contrasting plantings, rock outcrops and bodies of water each small garden typified one specific aspect of a natural landscape. Furthermore, the house and surrounding gardens were designed so that the plants used inside the house led the eye to the outside planting to give a sense of living in natural settings. The objective of these interrelated design elements was to create within a limited space a sense of the unique features of the natural landscape but integrated into an organic whole inside and out.

The garden picture thus provided clear and open spatial linkages between the observer or resident and the vividly presented scenes inside and out. These scenes changed as one changed his vantage point but all integrated into a sense of the unity of man and his natural world.

The furnishings within the house were carefully selected and placed to harmonize with the total ambience being sought in the overall design. Particularly important were watercolor paintings, waterbrush drawings and beautiful calligraphed poems hung either perpendicularly in pairs or singly in a horizontal axis on the walls. Thus, the beautiful outside scenes in harmony with the tranquil atmosphere inside the halls were designed to lead to a sense of repose and oneness with the living for resident and visitor alike. The gardening arts were one with the other arts and had as their end the celebration of man in a harmonious world.

Chinese gardening integrates the beauty of nature, architecture and mountains-and-water painting, which was created by Chinese artists to "link the outer beauty of nature with his inner artistic perceptions" To "draw" his pictures the Chinese garden designer used the same approach to build gardens.

Many Chinese painters and poets were accomplished gardeners. They deeply appreciated the sense of poetic flavor and picturesque scene which careful management of spatial layout could achieve. They were challenged by the problem of taking the original things of nature and creating a harmonious picture and the feeling of being in nature.

In the mid-8th century the Chinese techniques of gardening and drawing had passed to Japan. This cultural transfer process continued over the centuries. This continuing influence reached its high point at the end of the Ming Dynasty in the 17th century when a gardening expert, Chu Shun Shui, went to Japan to build the famous Hou Lu Yuan Garden in Tokyo. This garden made a deep impression on the Japanese and their garden style.

In the early 18th century, Chinese garden concepts reached England through William Chambers, who visited that country on two separate occasions. When requested to design the Kew Gardens for the Duke of Kent he incorporated elements of Chinese landscape design. Even today parts of the Kew Garden retain a sense of "Chinese style".

In 1981 at the request of the United States government and as a part of the Chinese/U.S. cultural exchange program a replica (called Ming Xuan — "bright veranda with windows") of one of Soochow's loveliest gardens was made in China and shipped to New York for exhibit at the Metropolitan Museum of Art. The model for this replica is the Wang Shi Yuan garden built during the early Southern Sung

Dynasty (12th century) in Soochow — and a typical Soochow garden. It is considered a classic expression of "seeing widely from the very small" and the epitome of a continuous, contrasting garden replicating nature.

General plane figure of Ming Xuan (Veranda with Windows) in Wang Shi Yuan Garden of Soochow.

The middle part of Wang Shi Yuan Garden.

Yi Yuan Garden.

2 *History of Chinese Gardening*

PREHISTORY, QIN (221–206 B.C.) AND EARLIER HAN (206 B.C.–A.D. 7) DYNASTIES

The history of Chinese gardening is one of continuing evolution from primitive beginnings 2200 years ago. Since the 11th century B.C. gardens and the gardening arts have been a continuing focus of Chinese cultural life. The growth and development of the concept of gardens was marked by periods of rapid change and evolution followed by periods of consolidation, but the distinctive qualities of Chinese gardening have remained constant.

The Chinese character for gardens is *You* or *Yuan.* It is first found in the famous ancient dictionary *Shuo Wen* written by Xu Zhen in the 2nd century. It means an enclosure in a natural forest to conserve birds and beasts and to be used as a hunting ground by kings.

The first such "garden" recorded in the Chinese pages of history is that of King Zhou Wen Wong established in the 11th century B.C. at Feng (Sian). The enclosure is reported to have been approximately 35 km in circumference. Confucius in *Shi Jing* (A Book of Songs) mentions three royal hunting grounds of "gardens": Lin Tai, Lin You and Lin Zhao located in Sian of Shensi province.

In the early 3rd century the idea of improving such natural areas to more closely reflect Chinese esthetic values is first documented. From these humble beginnings having to do with the chase, the concept of the garden as a human cultural undertaking emerged and was integrated into the Chinese cultural tradition. The first primitive gardens of which we know are the Yuan Pu of the Zheng Kingdom; Chong Tai of Qi Kingdom; Wu-Tong Yuan (Chinese parasol garden); and Hui Jing Yuan (landscape-assembled garden) of the Wu Kingdom.

Architectural constructions — halls, pavilions, corridors, bridges, etc. — which were to become one of the heading features of Chinese garden design were first incorporated into the Zhang Hue Yuan garden in the Cuo Kingdom. King Fu Cha of the Wu Kingdom built his Guan Wa Palace in a garden. This architectural assemblage had as its central focus an open corridor with rustling pendants and carved beams, painted rafters, copper gutters, and a jade banister situated before a lotus pond.

The unification of China (221 B.C.) under the Qin Dynasty opened a new era of political, economic and cultural development. The Chinese concepts of garden design shared in this cultural upsurgence. In Guanzhong (Central Shanzi Plain) palace/garden construction was carried out on a large scale with a particularly notable group of gardens built in Xian Yang, the capital of Shanzi at that time. Qin landscape design built upon the style received from the period of the Warring Kingdoms (403 — 221 B.C.). The buildings incorporated in the garden also followed Warring Kingdom patterns — halls, pavilions, lofts and bridges connecting terraces. The imperial garden also used bridges to connect the upper floors of the various buildings in the first palace compound. Subsequently, Lan Chi (Blue Pond) was excavated to form a large (100 × 10 km) lake in which was built on an island a stone hall, Peng Ying (Flourishing Sea). The lake was supplied by a canal dug from the Wei River. The most outstanding garden of this period was later constructed close to the Wei River. It is known as Shanglin Yuan (Upper Forest Garden) in which the well-known Afeng Palace was located.

The famous Chinese writer Du Mu (A.D. 803 — 853) provides us with this description of Afeng Palace:

> The Palace on Li Shan (Mountain) turned from North to West along a (150 km) way with pavilions and palaces hidden in the deep shade of trees. Pavilions and lofts were cunningly placed in accord with the rise and fall of the land and connected one to the other with artistic arcades. Creeks and streams flowed under long bridges or were crossed by high rainbow bridges. The palace was made even more beautiful when water was drawn from the Wei and Fan Rivers to extend and enlarge the lakes, ponds and water courses in the gardens.

The Han Dynasty boasted three emperors whose efforts made a significant contribution to the gardening arts of China. The first was the Emperor Han Gao Zu (from 5 B.C. to A.D. 7). He built two notable palaces — namely, Chang Le Palace in the southern part of Chang An City (now Sian) and later Wei Yang Palace in Sian. Probably the most important of the Han Dynasty emperors in terms of the development of gardens was Emperor Wu Di (A.D. 7 to 30). To celebrate his birthdays and to provide a proper site for Ying Xian (to welcome the coming of the celestials) he enlarged the Wei Yang gardens. Particularly notable were the three scenic islands: Peng Dai, Fang Zhang and Ying Zhou, which were built in the enlarged lake called Ta Ye Chi (Pond). He also renovated and enlarged the Shanglin Yuan of the Qin Dynasty. The enclave became not only the royal pleasure grounds but also the political and economic center of the Han empire. The grounds provided mountains and streams for the pursuit of hunting and fishing by the royal family and its entourage. Rare and exotic plants were brought in to inform and astonish visitors. Throughout the garden, fruit trees of all descriptions were planted to provide the court with an abundance of fresh fruit. The garden was so large, its topography so varied and its watercourses so extensive that it was used for the training of military and naval forces. To protect the Imperial Family and bureaucracy, sentry towers were placed at strategic positions around the 150 km circumference.

The Emperor Wu Di also built in the northern valley of Chang An, Gan Quan Yuan (Sweet Fountain Garden), constructed principally to view and enjoy mountain scenery. Halls, pavilions, lofts and bridges were built to enhance the view of particularly beautiful sites. Four lakes were constructed for boating. New garden features were incorporated such as a fountain spurting from the mouth of a copper dragon. In his book *Han Gong (Palaces of Han Dynasty)*, Ban Gu described the Gan Quan Yuan:

> Hills were piled up in the inner garden, rare trees planted on the slopes, streams from creeks filled all the pools. This garden masterfully integrated skilled craftsmanship with the beauty of nature.

Lian Xiao Wang, the second son of Emperor Wen Di, who was military governor of Sui Yang for a period of 35 years. built a large luxurious garden in his capital Sui Yang. This garden was named Dong Yuan (Eastern Garden). In addition to the extensive and beautiful traditional pavilions, halls and bridges, rockeries, caves and ponds with artificial islands were built. Waterfowl were introduced and encouraged to nest in the ponds.

In Han times the first gardens owned by private citizens emerged. The first such garden recorded is that of the wealthy merchant Yuan Guang Han, built at the foot of Bei Wang Shan in northeast Loyang.

The later Han Dynasty was a period of great turmoil and difficulty. The Emperor Liu Xiu was forced to remove his capital from Chang An to Loyang when the palaces and gardens were destroyed by the rebel Red-eyebrowed Armed Forces. Only two small Imperial palaces/gardens were built during later Han times. But strangely, as the difficulties of the Han increased, the position of eunuchs and high officials improved. Many of them, with their new-found wealth and influence built gardens, some of which in their splendor equalled the smaller royal gardens.

To summarize:

1. Royal gardens evolved from the primitive "enclosure" of King Zhou Wen Wong to the artificially enhanced garden (Yuan) of the Han Dynasty. In short, the concept of a garden as distinct from natural landscape was first appreciated.
2. The royal gardens were generally called "territory of palaces" meaning that the main focus of these early gardens were the courts, pavilions, halls, corridors, bridges and other architectural features.

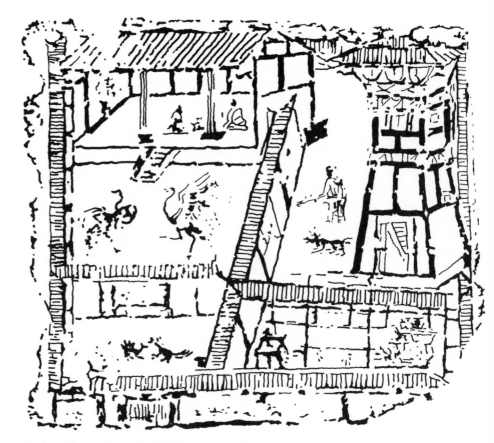

A drawing on the bricks of a private residence-garden in Han Dynasty of the 1st century.

Landscaping with plants, as we understand gardens, was still in a distinctly secondary position.

3. In Han times various groups of buildings were dedicated to specific uses such as Xuan Qu Gong (Palace) for playing music; Fu Li Guan (Hall) for cultivating tropical plants; Zou Ma Guan for raising horses; Yu Niao Guan for keeping birds and fishes.

4. The Han Dynasty marks a period of great creativity in gardening with the enhancement of natural topographic features; the introduction of artificial lakes and ponds fed by nearby streams and rivers; the careful consideration of local conditions in designing the garden and the development of various man-made constructions to enhance the beauty and interest of the garden.

5. Han times also saw the development and growth of the private, residential garden. The arts of gardening were no longer the exclusive preserve of the Imperial family and its entourage.

6. The concept of the garden was further enhanced by the notion of bringing artistic principles to bear on the design of gardens. The canons of Chinese landscape painting, which became a central Chinese cultural influence from Han times forward, were incorporated into the notions of how mountains, rocks, water, trees, flowers and traditional architecture should be disposed and correlated to incorporate beauty, significance and meaning into gardens.

WEI, JIN (A.D. 221 — 317), SOUTHERN AND NORTHERN (A.D. 317 — 581) SONG DYNASTIES

The 3rd to 6th centuries of Chinese history was a period of continuing warfare, turmoil and disorder. The period was typical of feudal societies. China was composed of many small warring states or factions which rose briefly to influence only to be displaced in continuing military confrontations with other states or factions reminiscent of the European Dark Ages. The old Northwest plains area, which had been the center of Han China, was overrun by barbarians forcing the native Chinese dynasties to flee to the South. Gardens were built, indeed some renowned gardens were first established in these difficult times and the gardening arts were advanced, but the period is not as notable as either Han or later dynasties nor have many documents dealing with gardens come down to us.

We know, for example, of the Dong Qiao (Copper Peacock) Yuan built in Nie Cheng City for the Wei Kingdom. But little is know of it other than its existence. More noteworthy was the Fang Lin (Fragrant Forest) Yuan built in a northern suburb of Nie Cheng City by Chang Lung, a talented landscape architect. This garden followed the best of the design principles developed by Han landscape designers.

The Wu Kingdom (222 — 280) was centered on the lower stretches of the Yangtse River. Favorable climatic conditions, beautiful natural settings, rich plant resources and ample water made this area especially suitable for exquisite gardens. Among the well known gardens were West Yuan, La Xin Yuan and Gua Lin Yuan.

The Western Jin (265 — 317) Emperor Si Ma Yan reconstructed Fang Lin Yuan and changed its name to Hua Lin (Lush Growth of Trees) Yuan. A notable private garden which lasted until Tang times was Jin Gu (Golden Valley) Yuan built for the wealthy Dan Chong. It was located in the Golden Valley and was completely surrounded by water.

At the beginning of the 4th century the royal family of the Western Jin moved from Loyang to Jian Kang (now Nanking) on the lower southern reaches of the Yangtse River. For this new capital they adopted the old name used in Loyang of Hua Lin Yuan for their palace/gardens. It was smaller than the former garden but was reportedly exquisite. Extensive plantations of citrus trees were established outside the walls, with pomegranate, weeping willows and Chinese scholar trees *(Sophora japonica)* lining the road through the Zhu Qiao Gate to the landscape area.

During the early Song Dynasty (420 — 479) three gardens were built which advanced in the gardening arts beyond the standards of the Hans. They were Le You (Happy Tourist) Yuan, Shang Lin (Upper Forest) Yuan and Nan (South) Yuan. Prince Xiao Chang Mian (483 — 502) was especially fond of landscape gardening, and established his Xuan Pu Yuan (Mysterious Garden) at the foot of Zhong Shan (Bell Mountain) in the eastern section of Taicheng City where the colourful buildings and grounds added a human dimension of beauty to the fascinating natural landscapes.

The Emperor Wu Di (from 535 to 543) was a strong supporter of Buddhism. He built the Dong Tai Temple (now Jimin Temple) in Nanking. The temple buildings were set in a splendid garden featuring rockeries and many water courses. It is one of the best known gardens of the period.

Other well-known gardens established during this dynasty were Nan Ping Wang's (King's) Tree Garden and Xian Dong Wang's South Garden of aquatic plants. These gardens had some of the characteristics of botanical gardens, as they are the first known to attempt to display a wide variety of both ornamental plants and fruit trees. While the author is intent only on providing a brief history of Chinese gardens, and not a philosophical treatise on the intellectual history of China, it should be pointed out that these two gardens marked a significant accretion to the emerging and developing concept of the garden. They were the first to treat the garden not only as an esthetic expression but also as a pedagogic undertaking. These two gardens mark the first consistent effort to acquaint garden visitors with the range of plants available for both ornamental and practical purposes which could be successfully cultivated in Nanking. The inclusion of this informational element significantly augmented the Chinese concept of the garden by expanding the notions of why gardens are made and what their objectives should be.

The gardens of the Southern Dynasties were traditionally noted for the excellent architectural complexes built within them. Unfortunately, we must accept the traditional views as these buildings were nearly all destroyed at the hands of the Hou Jing rioters during the reign of Jian Kang (from 583 to 589) in Nanking. The disastrous results have been described in this way:

> Looking to the west, Bo Van Yuan disappeared,
> trees withered, ponds dried,
> only ruins seen in the moonlight.

In addition to the Imperial Gardens, two noteworthy private gardens were built. One, Xie's Garden, built by Xie An was highly regarded not only for its esthetic layout but also for the extensiveness of its plant collection. The other, Cu's Garden, was designed by Gu Pi Jiang, a legendary landscape designer in Wu Jun City. However, these two gardens also disappeared — their ruins could not be located in Tang times.

Many talented scholars and retired courtiers turned to unconventional life styles during the period of the Southern Song Dynasties. A number of them retired to wild and remote places partly to escape an unruly society, but also from philosophical and religious convictions about the proper role of mankind. The gardening arts were intensively practiced by them. The interest of these highly placed individuals, in turn, made gardening fashionable in other sections of the society. Much of the prose and verse written by retired scholars dealt with landscapes and gardens, such as King Liang's *Tu Yuan Fu* (Rabbit Song), Fei Zi Ye's *Sightseeing Hua Lin Yuan* and Yu Sin's *Miniature Garden*. From this period henceforward, an appreciation of landscapes and the cultivation of gardens designed to reproduce landscape became an integral part of the high culture of China.

During the 53-year period from 907 to 960 when the North Central Plains were occupied by the five non-Han Nationalities, only a single garden was built in the Xiang Kingdom — Dan Lei's Sang Zi Yuan (from 941 to 957).

In the later Zhao Dynasty (from 951 to 959) Dan Hu restored the Wei Yang Palaces and gardens in Chang An City. To accomplish this enormous task he is reported to have drafted 260,000 male and female laborers to do the direct reconstruction work, while he forced another 160,000 to transport the 100,000 cartloads of building materials required to restore the tens of kilometers of walls, numerous buildings, rockeries and ponds. He is reported to have said "the morning the garden wall is completed, I would have had no regrets to die the same evening".

Emperor Dao Wu of the Northern Wei Dynasty (from 424 to 440) built a mountain resort surrounded by gardens north of the Great Wall at Sian. Although a retreat for the court, it was built along the lines of traditional formal imperial gardens.

The Da Lung Dun Yuan (Big Flying Dragon Garden) at Loyang built by the Emperor Mu Yong Xi of the Later Yan Kingdom (from 389 to 396) incorporated an artificial mountain which was styled after the mountain scenes of Jing Yun Shan. Water was drawn through a canal from Wu Chuan River to provide the waterscapes. This canal was later extended by Mu Rong Xu in Qu Guang Hai (sea) to create the artificial lakes Qu Quang Hai (Meander Sea) and Qing Liang Chi (Cool Pool).

These troubled times witnessed an enormous upsurgence in the practice of Buddhism among the people of Han. Not only the vastly increased number of the faithful but also the substantial support of imperial believers led to the building of great numbers of Buddhist Temples. Temples were frequently placed in locations of great natural beauty, in parallel with the movement of scholars and retired courtiers to such places. The natural attractiveness of the site of these temples was enhanced by the traditional Chinese arts of gardening. Thus, they became centers not only of worship by the faithful but also attracted sightseers and others in quest of beautiful spots in which to relax and contemplate. The frequent resort of the common people of China to these temples and their grounds did much to extend the appreciation of gardens and the gardening arts beyond the imperial circle and the ranks of the nobility. In this fashion the Buddhist temples contributed powerfully to the integration of gardens into the cultural tradition of China.

Several technical innovations in garden practice are also associated with the Buddhist Temple gardens. For example, the first water clock was installed at Ji Ming Temple in Nanking. The device was operated by a controlled flow of water dropping on the works from an overhead rock to count the passage of time. A golden statue of a water clock decorated the rock from where the water fell. From this time water clocks became a standard element of large Chinese gardens.

In looking back on this unhappy and tumultuous period of three centuries spanned by the three Kingdoms (Wu, Wei and Shu Han) and the Sixteen Kingdoms of the Five Tribes in the North, we can adduce the following about the concept and practice of the garden:

1. Despite the long periods of military confrontation between North and South and the economic privation caused by continuing warfare, some significant gardens were built.
2. People became weary of the unending disorder, riots and wars. They turned to religion and cultural pursuits to relieve the bleak conditions in which they lived. Scholars and retired court officials retreated to wild but naturally beautiful spots where they pursued the gardening arts in connection with practice of painting and literary writing. The common people turning in increasing numbers to Buddhism, frequented the temples and their gardens and so shared in the integration of gardening into the high culture of China.
3. The removal of the seat of the Han people government to the lower reaches of the Yangtse River had a favorable influence on the development of gardening. While the gardening practices were inherited from the Han Dynasty, the very favorable climate and soils of the Southern Empire permitted the making of spectacular gardens. Beyond this, the topography of South China is such that the many scenic and fascinating landscapes naturally available were quite advantageous to the development of gardens.
4. Chinese painting and literature pursued by the scholars and courtiers who had retired to remote and scenic spots turned upon "mountains and waters". The book *Ancient Paintings* written by Xie He in the 5th century emphasized six principles in painting: namely, atmosphere, layout, figure, color, site and modelling. These principles were integrated into the gardening arts of Southern China. In this way the Chinese esthetic tradition integrated both painting and gardening into the mainstream of Chinese culture.
5. With the introduction of exotic, rare, and useful plants into the practice of gardening for the expressed objective of informing visitors about the world of plants, the concept of gardening was expanded.

So while the 3rd to 6th centuries were extraordinarily difficult, the Chinese cultural tradition grew in stature and strength and the concept and practice of gardening was not only preserved but fully integrated into the Chinese cultural scene.

Scenes of Yi Yuan Garden.

CHINESE GARDENS IN SUI (A.D. 590 – 618) AND TANG (A.D. 618 – 906) DYNASTIES

In the last years of the 6th century, the difficulty and turmoil with which the Chinese had lived for three centuries was finally brought to an end. This remarkable achievement was brought about by the Chinese general Yang Guang who took the title of Emperor and founded the Sui Dynasty. The Sui dynasty came to an end with his meglomaniacal son who nearly lost the fruits of the Sui reunification of China. The situation was saved by Li Shil Min the founder of the illustrious Tang Dynasty, who in seven years of violent and intricate civil war destroyed all his numerous competitors and placed the stamp of a central, unified government on China which endures to the present.

The Tang Dynasty was one of the most profoundly and gloriously productive ages of cultural development and expression the world has witnessed. All of the arts excelled in this age of astonishing genius including the art of gardening. The first Sui Emperor, Yang Guang, undertook both the restoration of the Eastern Garden in the old traditional capital of Chang An and the establishment of the Xi Yuan (Western Gardens) in the western city of Loyang. To build the latter he appointed the talented garden designer, Hung Sheng. Hung constructed for the Emperor an elaborate and unusual labyrinth. This was a complex architectural structure of room and passageways going in and out, through turns and bends. At one moment a wanderer in the structure would find himself in a spot where he was confused as to direction and all seemed heavy and indistinct, but would then come upon, via a corridor, a place of unique beauty in a courtyard. Or he entered an inner room with no apparent way out, but by a hidden turn he would come upon the vista of a palace.

This ingenious structure was important in the development of the Chinese sense of appropriate garden design. The vistas presented by looking out of various windows, doors, passages, etc. were in all later times expected to present views of marked garden differences — here a waterscape, there a mountain view and beyond a flowering garden — all within a severly confined space, yet each appearing as a natural landscape.

The Emperors of the Tang Dynasty and particularly the remarkable Emperor Wu Chao built numerous splendid and well devised gardens. Rare and unusual specimens were collected to demonstrate the astonishing range of plants in this world. Recreational (ball playing grounds in particular), relaxation, contemplative and visual needs as well were all served by the rapid development of the concept of gardens and the ends they should serve.

In Sian the Emperor Yuan Zong, influenced by the example of the scholars of the previous period, a new perception of nature and tiring of the luxury, artifice and ostentation of the traditional court, built a remarkable series of gardens at the foot of Li Mountain. The best of the principles of garden design were utilized. A broad range of plants, both domestic and exotic, were carefully and cunningly planted around the extensive lakes and watercourses and on the piled up rockeries. The materials used in the extensive array of buildings — halls, lofts, corridors and pavilions — were for the first time left exposed and uncolored. The nature and color of the materials used were used to enhance the sense of nature and carry out human construction in accordance with the Tang perception of harmony with nature. Every effort was made to beautify the garden by carefully constructing the buildings in accord with the principles of nature and the site. In addition, the buildings were cunningly designed to present the occupants with ever-changing views of plants and landscapes as they moved from one room to another. The natural setting was enhanced by the careful siting and planting of trees, bushes and flowers. In short, the hand of both the gardener and the architect was not only to preserve but enhance the natural site selected.

But the Tang period is notable in the history of Chinese gardening not only for the new levels of excellence of design based upon a finely tuned and coherent view of the natural world and man's proper role in that world but also because it marked the extensive spread of private gardens constructed principally for high officials of the court. In earlier times a few private gardens had been built but they became common and widespread during this period.

It was during the Tang Dynasty that access to positions of authority in the Chinese political system first clearly came to depend upon high levels of achievement attained in official examinations. Scholars, poets and other young men who aspired to responsible positions in the court turned to a thorough training in the Chinese classics in preparation for the examination. Positions at court were assured to those who had done their homework well. As a consequence of this mode of recruitment, many officials were more remarkable as scholars, poets, calligraphers and artists than as servants of the court. Many of China's most notable cultural figures from this period forward spent their active years at court. As was pointed out earlier, the metaphysical views associated with Taoism and Buddhism led many of these scholar/officials as believers, to retire to relatively uninhabited scenic spots in the mountains or other remote places. The result was that gardening, one of the arts carried by these scholar/artist/officials to their places of retirement, led to the development of numerous residential gardens.

Thus we learn of the prime minister Li De Quan's splendid Ping Quan Zhang Yuan (Ping Quan Mountain Resort) from the description in his book *Plants and Rockeries in Ping Quan Mountain Resort*. The splendour of this garden is confirmed by the poet Bai Zu Yi who visited the garden three times yearly to savor its excellence and renew his spirit.

One of the outstanding painters and poets of China was Wang Wei. After his retirement from the Tang court he built his retreat Wang Chuan Bie Nie (Country Villa). He took advantage of the exquisite landscapes of Wang Chuan to conform his house and gardens to the canons of that school of Chinese landscape painting which favored scenes full of poetic flavor. Wang Wei was one of the first Chinese

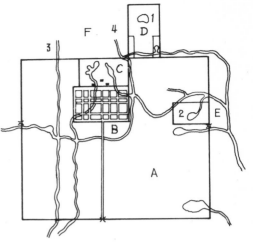

The imperial palace-garden of the Tang Dynasty, 7th–10th century.
A. outer city wall
B. imperial city
C. palace city
D. Da Min Palace
E. Shing Ching Palace
F. outside of city
1. Tai Yi Chi (Tai Yi Pong)
2. Long Cheng (Dragon City)
3. Li Yuan (Pear Garden)
4. Jin Cheng (Forbidden City)

artists to thoroughly articulate and record the traditional Chinese esthetic which integrates the arts of poetry, calligraphy, painting and gardening. The four arts in one reflects the Chinese perception of the harmony of proper human undertakings with the operation of the natural world.

The poet Bai Zu Yi, already mentioned, is one of China's most revered and read poets. Upon his retirement from a long and distinguished career in the service of the Tang, he chose a naturally scenic spot at Lu Shan on which to construct his residence. Here he constructed a simple house, Kuang Lu (Rectified House). In a letter to a friend he described the surroundings as follows: "Xiang Lo Shan (Incense Mountain) lies in the west to east forests of Lu Shan. It is a good habitat for many rare plants. The wonderful rocks, the clear waters in creeks and ponds, the magnificent aged trees, all in all, everything was attractive, so I had a simple house built which quite satisfied." He continued, "In front of my residence there are aged pines and deep green bamboo groups, clear creeks flow nearby with natural slab bridges to get across, trailing plants form a natural hedge around my home. Really it is a unique place for me to work, relax and enjoy."

The feudal society of the Sui (590 – 618) and Tang (618 – 906) Dynasties were among the most illustrious in all Chinese history in terms of their cultural achievements, not the least of which were the extent, number and quality of their gardens.

The contribution of this period to the gardening arts of China may be summarized as follows:

1. Palace-gardens which heretofore emphasized architectural structures set in natural surroundings began to turn to the controlled enhancement of the setting, through the careful use of gardening arts. This development marked a turning point in garden history. The precepts of gardening articulated in this period were accepted as traditional and were maintained and extended in the later periods of the Ming (1368 – 1644) and Qing (1644 – 1912) Dynasties and indeed up to present times.

2. The canons and criteria of Chinese landscape painting were formalized during Tang times. These formulations involved:
   a) the correct laying out of the scene in space
   b) the proper arrangement of the principle objects of the painting to place them in outstanding positions
   c) arrangement of objects to give the feeling of depth
   d) the importance of incorporating the metaphysical view of the ultimate harmony of nature and the proper role of man in conforming to and supporting this harmony

These formulations were and are viewed simply as the compilation or summation of traditional precepts and methods which finally received full recognition and expression in Tang times. The landscape paintings and garden designs of Wang Wei and Bai Zu Yi, two of China's leading artist-poet-calligrapher-gardeners epitomizes the fundamental and elemental patterns incorporating this canon. Chinese landscape design was conceived as being an integral element embodying the same metaphysics and views. Later scholar/officials concurred in the soundness and correctness of this canon and perception and by doing so confirmed the rectitude of the tradition.

3. During the Song (960 — 1126) Dynasty a book entitled *Gardens of Loyang* was written down from the memory of an old resident. The book tells of 20 gardens in the ancient capital. The gardens were of three kinds: flower gardens, recreation gardens and residence gardens. All were located on the outskirts of the city. This book represents the earliest record devoted exclusively to the development of Chinese gardens.

4. While the palace gardens of the Tang resembled the traditional gardens of Qin and Han times, the total area used was smaller while the standards of both architecture and gardening were markedly improved.

SONG (960 — 1126) AND YUAN (1279 — 1368) DYNASTIES

The chaotic, warring period of the Five Dynasties (907 — 960) was brought to a close by the pacific formation of the Song Dynasties (960 — 1126). The capital was established at Bianjing (now Kaifeng in Honan Province). South and east of Bianjing, the traditional capital (Beijing)· was vacated as the territory below Bianjing and the Great Wall had been lost to northern nomadic tribes during the anarchic Five Dynasties. The Song Dynasty is viewed by historians as the high point of traditional Chinese culture. Not surprisingly, the arts of gardening were not only advanced within the context of traditional imperial gardens but also in the widespread development of private gardens among the urban citizens of China.

The first imperial garden created in Bianjing was Qiong Lin Yuan which centered on a large artificial lake drawing water from the King River. In short succession, three additional imperial gardens were created, namely, Yi Chun Yuan, Yu Jing Yuan and Fang Lin Yuan. These early Song gardens are generally called "Four Gardens of the Song Dynasty".

The Song Emperor Zhao Ji (from 1082 to 1135) was devoted not only to painting, calligraphy and poetry, but gardening as well. He appointed two talented garden designers, Zhu Main and his son, to design a garden. This garden became known as the magnificent Gen Yue Yuan (Gorgeous Mountain Resort) on Gen Yue Mountain. Six years were required for its completion. In addition to the traditional structures, buildings, bridges and pavilions, the garden boasted an especially rich collection of plants widely gathered from throughout China and a remarkable collection of rocks (to build not only hills but also waterfalls, etc.) collected from Kiangsu and Chekiang Provinces.

In the meantime private gardens proliferated. The first recorded in the Song Dynasty was that of Fu Bi. The garden was notable in turning its back on the traditional extensive form of gardening to concentrate upon shaping garden scenes to present the appearance of great depth by using a winding fashion of design. From the same period we have records of another private garden famed for its waterscapes — Dong Yuan designed by its owner Wen Yan Bu.

The early decade of the 12th century brought a reduction in the extent of the Song empire as the nomadic Turkish and Mongolian tribes occupied the central plains of China. As a consequence, Jian Kang (now Nanking) became a secondary capital of the Southern Song Dynasty. A former garden spot Qing Xi Jiu Qu (Nine-Bend Blue Creek) was repaired. It was also modified to a waterscape garden within which an ancestral temple, Xian Xian Ci and some associated pavilions were relocated on an island by the division of a stream to create the island. The garden was noted for the abundant and colorful lotus flowers which encircled the island.

Shortly after the rebuilding of Jian Kang, the Southern Song was forced to remove its capital yet again to Lin An (now Hangchow) in the face of the unrelenting onslaught of the nomadic tribes. Another imperial garden was established, Yu Jing Yuan on the north face of Nan Long Shan (Nine Dragon Mountain). The artificial lake and man-made mountain are extant and can be viewed by the modern visitor.

The west Lake of Hangchow, developed in Tang times, had long been a famous scenic area. When the Song official, Bai Zu Yi, was placed in charge of Hangchow Prefecture, he added a reservoir. The dam or dike forming the reservoir was augmented by his successor Su Dong Po and named Su Di (dike) which remains one of the memorable scenes of West Lake to this day. With the move of the capital of the Southern Song Dynasty to Hangchow, West Lake became a primary focus of the new capital. By the time of the move to Hangchow (1127) all traditional "ten scenic spots of West Lake" had been completed. Ping Hu Qiu Yue (Autumn Moon on the Calm Lake) has long been considered the most beautiful view of the entire lake. Wang Hu Ting (Pavilion for Viewing the Lake) built during Tang times was reconstructed along the lakeside. Three islets graced the lake joined by the Nine Bend Bridge. The edge of the lake is marked by weeping willows underplanted with a variety of herbaceous flowers back dropped by the pavilions and terraced halls set in the surrounding green hills.

In the meantime the Liao Kingdom of the North set up its southern capital at Gui De in Honan Province. In imitation of Chinese cultural practice, a garden named Su Yuan was built. In addition and not to be outdone, the Jin Kingdom (Kin Kingdom) of the central plains established its capital at Beijing. They built the Da Min Palace which exists today, renamed as the Summer Palace. the garden in which the Summer Palace was set, Su Yuan, is now the North Sea of Beijing.

The remnants of the splendid Song Dynasty were finally extinguished by the devastation of the Mongolian invasion. In 1210 this ruthless tribe led by the notorious Genghis Khan attacked and conquered first the Kin and then the Liao Empires, leaving the Mongols in possession of the utterly devastated Northern Provinces of China. The Southern Song finally collapsed in 1279 leaving the

Mongols, under the adopted name of the Yuan Dynasty, firmly in control of all the lands of the Han. Fortunately, the brutal massacre of people and destruction of institutions which characterized the early years of the invasion in the Northern Provinces were mitigated as the invaders moved South and fell under the influence of the great and firmly rooted Chinese cultural traditions. Officially the Yuan Dynasty began with the accession of Kublai Khan in 1263. The Mongols to the west who had adopted Islam refused to recognize Kublai as their Mongolian overlord. So, isolated from tribal brethren to the west, the Mongols occupying China adopted in the fullest measure the Chinese cultural traditions.

The change of color of the Mongols in China is nowhere better marked that in the construction of the man-made lake Tai Ye Chi and man-made mountain Longevity Hill shortly after setting up their capital at Beijing. Only 35 years before Genghis Khan had vowed to level all of China in order to provide pasture lands for Mongolian horses. His successors in less than two generations were building gardens in the Chinese style, for the Tai Ye Chi and Longevity Hill were consciously patterned after the precepts of the Song landscape paintings.

Several private gardens dating from Yuan times are extant today — notably the Lion Grove in Soochow reknowned for its fine rockeries and the famous Huan Xiu Mountain Resort in Soochow. Both of the gardens were carefully maintained during the succeeding centuries and can be visited in our times.

The 400-year period spanning these two dynasties may be summed up in the following way:

1. The canon of the gardening arts, first fully formalized during the Tang Dynasty, was further refined and developed during the Song and Yuan Dynasties.
2. The Song Emperor Huizong was, and is, renowned as one of China's outstanding artists, whose work with brush — painting and calligraphy were characterized by delicate brushwork and close attention to detail. He gathered together the leading artists and calligraphers from throughout the Empire to form an elite group established in the Imperial Art Academy. The styles produced by the Emperor and the artists of the Academy set a traditional pattern of landscape painting which, in turn, markedly influenced landscape gardening practices. The gardens of the Song Dynasty were subsequently called "scholars pictures of mountains-and-waters". The gardening techniques involved in the planning and layout of rocks, piling-up of hills, excavating lakes, designing rockeries and planting of trees, bushes and shrubs were raised to a new and finer level.
3. Mathematics and physics were extensively pursued during the Song Dynasty. As a consequence, garden architecture incorporated the new technical innovations derived from these fields. These new approaches are recorded in the book "Building Methods in Song Dynasty". Garden design incorporated the newly developed principles of civil engineering in the construction of traditional halls, pavilions, corridors, bridges, temples, lakes, built-up hills, water courses, etc.

Landscape design became not only more realistic but was thoughtfully harmonized with the new styles in landscape paintings as well.

4. In keeping not only with the new appreciation of naturalism or realism in garden design but also a better appreciation of the environmental demands of plants, advantage was taken of natural habitats. Thus, climbers were grown on cliffs, plum trees were planted in ravines, pines and cypresses were located at the foot of piled-up hills, willows were located beside waterways and waterfalls formed by directing the flow of creeks over strategically placed rocks.

5. Plant material was collected from a wide variety of sources to include not only ornamental but also medicinal and edible plants for the instruction of visitors. These concerns for establishing natural environments for plants and the display of a wide variety of plant material for pedagogic purposes mark the beginnings of the true botanic garden.

6. Private gardens became a regular feature of Chinese culture starting in the capital Lin An of the Southern Song Dynasty. The West Lake area was richly endowed with splendid natural plant resources and scenic spots which were used to site many private gardens. The plants commonly planted in private gardens included sweet scented osmanthus, lotus, cottonrose hibiscus, ginkgo and willows. Peonies and hibiscus were reserved for use in the imperial gardens to enrich and set off these gardens.

MING (1368 – 1644) AND QING (1644 – 1912) DYNASTIES

The Ming Dynasty (1368) was established by Zhu Yuan Chang, who selected Nanking as his capital where he had built his palace-garden. It was planned on a larger scale and was more splendid and magnificent than those in Loyang. He reduced the position of Da Dou (Big Capital) to the Peiping Prefecture and appointed his son Zhu Di governor of Yan (Norther Heibei Province). Upon Zhu Yuan Chang's death, Zhu Di succeeded to the throne and removed the capital to Beijing. He undertook a major reconstruction of the old capital as part of a planned enlargement of the city's boundaries. His palace-garden, Xi Yuan (West Gardens) was built upon and around the existing lake Tai Ye Chi and Peng Lai Shan (now Qiong Hua Islet) with a Moon Hall at the top of it, which were originally constructed in the Jin Dynasty (1115 – 1234). The exquisite pavilions and halls on the islet were built during the Yuan Dynasty and included the three Big Temples: Ning He, Jin Cui and Tai Su. Trees, flowers and rocks were planted on the lakeside. A unique feature of the reconstructed lake scene was a jade dragon on one side of the lake from which jets of water sprayed into the lake while from a stone dragon on the opposite side of the lake water was sprayed downward like a waterfall in concert with the jets from the dragon. Another royal garden was located on the western outskirts called Hao Shan Yuan (Good Mountain Resort). It was based on the existing Yuan Jing Si (Seclusion Temple) of Lady Lou and is now known as the Summer Palace in Beijing.

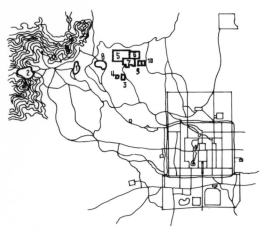

The imperial palace-gardens of the Ming and Qing Dynasties, 14th–20th century.
1. Jing Ming Yuan
2. Jing Ni Yuan
3. Chang Chun Yuan
4. Si Hua Yuan
5. Yuan Ming Yuan
6. Chang Chun Yuan
7. Mo Chun Yuan
8. Qing Yi Yuan
9. Jin Chun Yuan
10. Xi Chun Yuan

In addition to the imperial palace-gardens, a large number of private gardens were built in the city of Nanking. The private gardens were mostly located in the southwest section of the city. Hsu Da's Dong Yuan (East Garden) has traditionally been regarded as the best of the private gardens. The private gardens built along the lower reaches of the Yangtse River during the Ming Dynasty have been maintained to this day. Among the best known are Cho Zheng Yuan and Lui Yuan in Soochow, Chi Chang Yuan in Wusih, Yu Yuan in Shanghai and Zhan Yuan in Nanking.

At the end of the Ming Dynasty, the Hong Guang regime temporarily established its capital at Nanking. The most famous garden of that period was Yuan Da Cheng's Dan Chao Ju (Stone-nestle Residence). His friend Ji Chang, a talented garden-designer planned this residence-garden for him. Ji subsequently wrote the book *Arts of Gardening* which is the oldest gardening book of China. He systematically summarized both the theory and practice of gardening as developed in the gardens of the south located on the lower reaches of Yangtse River. Yuan supported him financially while writing the manuscript and later published the book for him. This classical gardening book was passed on first to Japan where it lay the theoretical foundations for that country's remarkable gardens. The book ultimately made its way to the countries of the West where it exerted a profound influence on the formal gardens of Europe.

The capital of the Qing Dynasty was established in Beijing. Its imperial garden, located outside of Ning Kun Gate, was formerly the backyard-garden of the Ming Dynasty which was renovated and extended into the Xi Yuan (West Garden). At the same time the Tai Yi Chi (lake) was also dredged and extended into North Sea, Middle Sea and South Sea, commonly called the Three Seas of Beijing. A white pagoda was erected in Qing Hua Islet.

The Jehol Provisional Palace was built at the Imperial Mountain Resort between 1702 − 1792. It was an architectural treasure with beautifully landscaped gardens. In addition, it was a symbol of the Qing policy of political and religious unification with the several nations bordering China on its northern and western frontiers. The architectural styles of the buildings included the Han, Mongolian and Tibetan. The religious traditions provided for, included Chinese Buddhism, Tibetan Lamaism, and Mohammedanism. The regional styles of landscape gardening were replicated as well. All in all, it was a tour de force of architecture, landscape design and politicocultural policy.

The succeeding reigns of the Emperors Kang Xi, Yung Cheng and Qian Long represented the Qing Dynasty at its most extensive and brilliant. It was a time of consolidating the best of traditional Chinese cultural. So it was that Kang Xi started the palace with a square courtyard characteristic of North China. Several of these gardens were copies of famous gardens of Central China. After his inspection of the south lower reaches of Yangtse River he adopted the architectural layout of landscape gardening typical of this area. He extended the 36 scenes in the resort to 72 scenes, among them the 3 pavilions on a lotus lake were modeled after the 5 pavilions at Shou Xi Hu (Thinnish West Lake) in Yangchow: the Misty Rain Pagoda from Yan Yu Lou, on Yuang Yang Dao (Mandarin Duck Islet) in Nan Hu (South Lake) of Jiaxing County near Shanghai; and the Jing Shan Dao (Golden Hill Islet) from Jing Shan of Zhen Jiang. This massive garden was completed during the reign of Kang Xi's grandson, the Emperor Qian Long. The Imperial Mountain Resort at Chengde (provincial capital of Jehol) remains the largest garden in China to this day and has long been well known in the world.

The Chang Chun Yuan located in Yuan Ming Yuan was built on the site of the abandoned private residential garden of Li Wei. The Yuan Ming Yuan on its north was originally bestowed upon Yong Zheng by his father the Emperor Kang Xi when Yong was king of the vassal state. After succeeding to the throne, he followed his predecessor, the Emperor Kang Xi in remodelling his garden along the lines of the gardens in the south lower reaches of Yangtse River. He used the designs of Lion Grove in Soochow, Xian You Tian Yuan (Little Heaven Garden) in Hangchow, and An Lang Yuan in Hai Nin. He invited a number of foreign architects to reconstruct this garden.

Yuan Ming Yuan had three gardens: "Yuan Ming Yuan", "Chang Chun Yuan" and "Wan Chun Yuan". They covered 350 hectares. In the Northern section of Chang Chun Yuan (Forever Spring Garden) were a group of European palaces in baroque and rococo styles. They were designed and built under the supervision of F. Giuseppe Castiglione, an Italian missionary and painter then working at the Qing Court, and two Frenchmen, P. Michaél Benoist and Jean Deni Attiret, during the reign of Emperor Qian Long (1736 — 1796).

The palatial building, Xie Qi Qu, was constructed of marble, which was then carved. Columns were decorated with flower scrolls and rows of leaves in Western Classical and Renaissance styles. Windows, balustrades and staircases were reminiscent of Versailles. The walls were mounted with multicolored glazed bricks and the roof topped with purple tiles.

On each side of the main facade were two octagonal pavilions. A fountain faced the mansion. In front of Hai Yan Tang (Hall), P. Benoist built a marvelous fountain clock. Twelve bronze animals were erected along the sides of a man-made pond to symbolize the different times of day and night according to the Chinese practice. Water gushed from the mouth of each animal corresponding to the time of day. Each animal would spray water for two hours a day and thus, a miraculous clock, working without pause for winding was formed.

Trees and bushes were planted and pruned in geometrical patterns in accordance with European fashion. Hedges, paths and sculptures imitated Western style.

At the southern end on the axis, across the Yuan Ying Guan (Hall), stood another group of European buildings — the miniature courtyard Guan Shui Fa — which was used by the Emperor to enjoy the sight of the fountain. It included a beautifully decorated stone throne, and two lateral entrances built in pure baroque fashion. Behind the throne was a four leaf stone screen carved in exquisite relief and two tiny quadrangle pagodas. The throne was covered by a canopy and flanked by two bronze cranes with outstretched wings.

The priceless relics and scriptures preserved in the garden were looted and the garden razed to the ground by the Eight-Power Allied Force which invaded Beijing in 1860.

The Empress Dowager (1835 — 1908) reconstructed her palace-garden Yi He Yuan (now the Summer Palace) on a part of the burned site. She appropriated 30,000,000 taels of silver (= $15,000,000) originally allotted for rebuilding the Chinese Navy to restore the palace garden.

A number of the notable gardens in Nanking were heavily damaged by the Qing as they overrode the falling Ming Dynasty in the south of China. Many of these gardens were rebuilt in Qing times. Emperor Qian Long rebuilt a garden named Sui Yuan in Nanking which was designed and built down the side and along the foot of Xia Cong Shan (hill). The halls were constructed on the higher slope while the pavilions and small bridges were built in a half circle at the base of the hill so the scene could be easily appreciated from the hall. Ornamental plants were artfully placed so that in all seasons the garden was aflame with the color of the plants blooming in their season — peonies in the spring, osmanthus in autumn and so on.

Added to the remarkable gardens of Nanking was the "Heavenly Garden" built under the direction of the "Heavenly King", Hong Xiu Quan, the leader of the Tai Ping rebellion. This religious rebellion, based on Christianity, originated in the southern city of Canton and threatened in the mid-19th century to overthrow the Qing Dynasty. The Tai Ping Heavenly Kingdom established its capital at Nanking. The site of a nunnery, Miao Xiang, was selected as the foundation for the garden. The garden is notable for its extensive plantings of flowering plants and bamboos planted in groups around the columned halls and pavilions.

Yangchow, an ancient cultural and commercial city of south-eastern China since the Sui and Tang Dynasties is the location of another notable assemblage of gardens. When the Qing Dynasty came to power there were already eight famous gardens and four well-known temples located in the city. Emperor Qian Long visited Yangchow six times and added to its splendid gardens. In addition, many high officials built their residence-gardens there. The Yangchow gardens were particularly noted for their splendid rockeries which resulted from the skillful architecture used in their placing. The most notable rockeries were designed by leading painters. Thus, Yu's Mo Dan Yuan (Ten thousand Stone Garden) was planned by the famous artist Ceng Tao; the Jian Cun Rockgarden by Chang Nan Heng; Xuan Dan Shan (hill) by Chou Hao; and Nine Lion Rock Hill by Dong Dao.

Most of these well known rockeries and rockgardens were located in the Rainbow Bridge area. On the west embankment of Rainbow Bridge were the highly regarded spots "Chang Di Chun Luo" (Spring Willow on Long Embankment), and "Si Qiao Yan Yu" (Misty-rain Four Bridge). On the east embankment is found the scenic spot, Jiang Yuan, well known for its rockeries. On islets in the Shou Xi Hu (Lake) of Rainbow Bridge there are two gardens: Da Hung Yuan and Xiao Hung Yuan, both designed by the famous garden designer Zhou Shu Qiu. On the north outskirts of Yangchow the Dong Yuan of Tian Nin Temple is remarkably representative of the garden style of the Qing Dynasty with its aged plum trees, trees, ponds, bridges, rocks, rockeries, waterfalls and fountains combined in careful ways to present a series of splendid garden scenes.

Emperor Qian Long assigned to Kao, the Censor of the Court, the responsibility for the construction of a new canal, the Lian Hua Geng Canal. The canal linked Thin West Lake to Ping Shan Hall. Many private gardens were built on both sides of the canal. The famous Lian Hua Qiao (bridge) was built not only to span the canal but also to provide five pavilions designed to view the scene from different perspectives. The bridge was built to connect gardens on both sides of Thin West Lake to Ping Shan Hall. The latter was originally built by the famous Song Dynasty poet-writer, Ouyang Xiu. Unfortunately, this historic and noted scenic spot and the other outstanding gardens of Yangchow were all destroyed during the war between the Taiping Revolutionary Army and the Qing Dynasty. After the Taiping rebels were subdued, several of the most beloved sites were rebuilt including Lu Yang Tsun (Green Willow Village), Shou Xi Hu (Thinnish West Lake), Five Pavilion Bridge and Ping Shan Dong. The rebuilt gardens have been maintained carefully since then and can be viewed by today's visitor.

Soochow has long been renowned for its beautiful landscapes and classical gardens. From generation to generation, many scholars, talented garden designers, skilled garden craftsmen and experienced gardeners settled in the city. They were drawn to the city by virtue of its fame as a city of gardens and aspired to enhance its reputation. The most notable contributors to the classical Soochow gardens were Zhu Chong, and his son Zhu Mian; Chang Lian; Shen Mo San; and Gu Ya Yin. In many cases, descendants of these landscape artists carried forward their work in the traditional arts of Chinese gardening.

The classical gardens of Soochow were scattered through the city. The most notable were Tsang Lang Ting (Translucent Pavilion) of the Song Dynasty; Lion Grove of the Yuan Dynasty; Zhuo Zheng Yuan (Humble Political Opinion Garden) of the Ming Dynasty and Liu Yuan of the Qing Dynasty. These gardens have traditionally been perceived as a group and hence were called the Four Gardens of Soochow. A number of private gardens in the classical style added to Soochow's reputation as the center of classical gardening in China. The best known include Huan Xiu Shan Zhuang (Beautiful Mountain Surrounded Villa) and Yi Yuan (Cheerful Garden). The finest private garden undoubtedly was Wang Shi Yuan which was originally the site of Shi's Mo Juan Tang (Ten Thousand Books Library). According to the *Chronicle of Soochow Prefecture* the number of private gardens reached 200 in the three counties of Wu Xian, Chang Zhou and Uyan He under the jurisdiction of Soochow Prefectural Government. Unfortunately, the ravages of time and neglect have worked their inevitable way so that only a few of the these fine gardens exist today.

The palace gardens of the Ming and Qing Dynasties constitute the most glorious chapter in Chinese gardening history. Their features can be summarized as follows:

1. The palace gardens of the Ming and Qing Dynasties refined the theory and practice of the traditional gardening arts, first clearly developed in the Tang, Song and Yuan Dynasties. In them, many feel the Chinese garden reached its highest peak of perfection. The free layout of landscapes cunningly replicated natural scenes. Indeed the objective of the landscape artists was to capture the essence of the natural order. This approach differed markedly from the geometric-tidy style of gardening in the West. In order to take advantage of the natural beauty of mountains and waters, the imperial palace gardens of the Ming and Qing Dynasties were built on the outskirts of the capital and were designed to be harmonious with the conditions of the site.

2. By the end of the Ming Dynasty, a number of private gardens flourished around the Tai Hu (lake) in Peijing where the green mountains and clear water surface were visible from every vantage point. Most private gardens were located within the walls of the city and so were built on a necessarily small scale but were marked by exquisite design and construction. All private gardens surrounded the residence of their owner.

3. The garden styles of North China were much influenced by the introduction of the garden designs originating in the south along the lower reaches of the Yangtse River. This style had developed out of the tradition of private southern residential gardens. This southern, private garden style exerted a major influence on the construction of imperial palace gardens from Ming times forward.

4. The garden style of the West had, by Ming times, reached China. It did, in fact, influence Chinese practices — witness the European buildings and designs incorporated in the Yuan Ming Yuan, for example.

5. Some of the gardens built in the Ming and Qing Dynasties were sufficiently well kept that they exist today. These gardens now represent some of the highest achievements of the gardening arts of China. They, together with the garden books written during the Ming and Qing Dynasties, provide the example and instruction by which the Chinese landscape traditions are kept alive to our day. The imperial palace gardens, in the form of the Summer Palace in Beijing and the Chengde Mountain Resort in Jehol, together with the Four Gardens in Soochow represent the high point of the unique and splendid tradition of the gardening arts of China.

With this brief history we have tried to trace the main outlines of the development of the concept of the garden in China. From its origins 2000 years ago, as a natural area set aside as the hunting grounds for the Imperial family and its attendants within which were located the Imperial residences, to the carefully and artfully designed gardens of Ming and Qing, several consistent and constant themes can be discerned. These themes and their historic development resulted in a coherent body of theory and practice which have informed not only the design of Chinese gardens but those of Japan and to some degree the landscaping principles incorporated in modern western gardens.

Scene of Yi Yuan Garden.

The principles upon which the mature concept of the Chinese garden arts rest may be briefly summarized as follows:

1. Mankind is embedded in the Natural Order as an active though not dominant player.
2. Man's role in the Natural Order is not to impose his will on Nature but rather to assist in the expression of that which is appropriate to the Natural Order of things. This contrasts markedly with the traditional western view that Man is free to reconstruct the natural order according to his views.
3. It is, therefore, incumbent upon Man to understand the inner expression and meaning of natural phenomena and enhance and assist that expression and meaning. Thus, a favorite expression of Chinese esthetic is that of the Sage who spends thirty years in a wild and rude place observing bamboo and then returning to paint in ten brush strokes the essence of bamboo.
4. The art of Chinese gardening and the arts of Chinese painting, calligraphy and poetry spring from common esthetic principles. All aim to express and rejoice in the harmony of the natural order. The gardening arts were regarded as coequal with and of importance equal to what in the West are called the fine arts.
5. Essential to every garden are rocks (the skeleton of the world), water (the blood of the world), plants (the clothing of the world) and harmonizing architectural construction (adaptation to the needs of man).
6. The garden is the concentration or storehouse of the plants of the world. This precept of collecting as many species as possible in a small space to inform man of the multitudinous variety of the Natural Order is a theme which was by the time of Frederic II of Sicily evident in western garden theory and practices. This approach to garden practice was clearly the product of the Chinese tradition as received in the West and now embodied in the concept of the botanic garden.
7. Appropriately sited and designed architectural constructions — residence hall, pavilions, bridges, etc. — were from the beginning considered to be essential to a garden. Much of the grace of traditional Chinese architectural theory and practice grew out of the practice of designing buildings so that they fit harmoniously in the landscape.
8. The western sense of indoors versus outdoors was foreign to the Chinese concept of landscape design practice. The building and its furnishings were meant to carry the sense of the exterior scenes into the building and so into the sensibilities of the building's occupants.
9. The garden must be planned and laid out to give the viewer, whether in the garden itself or in a building in the garden, continuously changing and varied insights into the natural world.

3 *The Art of Design*

The essential design principles incorporated in Chinese gardening are: a dynamic layout of the elements (siting of plants, paths, watercourses, rockeries, etc.); remodelling of the garden's topography to one consistent with nature; and the inspiration and pleasure to be found in mountains, water and forests. These principles are creatively realized in the contrast of ever-changing scenes as the viewer walks through the garden or moves from one room to another in the building which is located within the garden. In the hands of an inspired designer these objectives could be realized and coordinated within the constraints imposed by the natural lay of the land, local growing conditions and the plant species selected.

TOPOGRAPHICAL OBSERVATION AND ORIENTATION

China, a country of vast territory, was blessed by Mother Nature with gorgeous mountains and waters, natural features often used as sources of inspiration by many of China's leading poets. However, it is the Chinese view that natural landscapes can be further beautified through the application of the creative and skillful craftsmanship of man. Gardens were and are established in natural scenic spots, first of all. The garden is conceived as an integral part of its native setting. It is an additional scenic spot, harmoniously integrated into the natural landscape. In a well-known lyric poem this concept is articulated as: "Whose pavilion topped the green mountains, the only red spot". This passage encapsulates the traditional idea that the subtly and carefully positioned pavilion not only provided a bird's-eye view of the entire scene, but was also the finishing touch required to complete the total esthetic harmony of the scene — a touch which only man inspired by a proper understanding of the natural order of things could provide.

27

The correct solution of the problem of topography is a constant in Chinese landscape design. Not only are gardens to be set in sites of natural scenic beauty but also they are expected to reveal or summarize the major topographic features present on earth. The latter sense is summed up in the phrase "A miniature world formed by itself". As an example of this line of thought, consider the numerously interwoven branches of an aged tree in the classical garden Lui Yuan of Soochow. The aged tree was the object, and the corridor placed opposite was so placed to appreciate this aged tree. In another classical garden, Zheng Zheng Yuan, "a pavilion to see the rockeries far-off" was used to observe in their fullness the rockeries on the opposite side with a watercourse serving as the foreground. These topographic considerations dominated not only the thinking underlying the Imperial gardens but private residential gardens as well.

From ancient times, both Buddhist monasteries and Taoist temples were usually located near or in forests or mountains. The objective in siting these sacred buildings in such locations was twofold. First, they were clearly separated from the common social life and could thereby signify their unique function. Secondly, they identified with the natural order of things inherent in such sites. Gardens constituted an integral element of these temples situated in natural landscapes. The best known are Beijing's Azure-cloud Temple, Hangchow's Ling Yin Sze (temple), Nanking's Qi Shia Sze, Zhen Jiang's Jin Shan Sze and Yangchow's Da Min Sze. Others are Omei Shan (High-steep Mountains) in Szechuan, Jiu Hua Shan in Anhwei and Pu Tuo Shan in Chekiang. These temples and monasteries are examples of traditional exquisite architecture located in picturesque natural sites and landscaped in a variety of styles. Typically their sites include flowing water, mountains, deep forests, lush plant growth, creeks, huge rocks, aged trees, deep caves and historic monuments. Many of China's outstanding gardens are closely related with famous temples and monasteries, located near gorgeous mountains and rivers or lakes.

There are many scenic spots and gardens along Dian Chi (a lake 150 km in circumference) in Kunming of Yunnan Province. One of the outstanding is the famous Da Quan Lou (tower). It is well positioned to view the scenes around the entire lake, the gorgeous far-off mountains, the endless reeds, the wild ducks floating on the water and eagles circling in the sky — all the variety and beauty of nature in one's sight from the tower.

The Wu Long Sze (Black Dragon Temple) located at Lo Shan in Szechuan Province is another well-sited temple. One side faces the awesome peak of Omei Shan while the other three sides look out upon the river which surrounds the tower. The architecture and gardens add the finishing touch to the beautiful landscape. The aged pines and native plants grow densely both in the front and back courtyards. It seems like a green carpet mounted by an ancient temple floating on the river.

The siting and gardening principles and effects of traditional Chinese landscape design were not confined to sacred settings. Secular gardens shared the same concepts. So the West Lake of Hangchow is particularly noted for its splendid views. Architectural structures are well coordinated with natural scenes. For example, Ping Hu Qiu Yue (Autumn Moon on the Calm Lake), at the southeastern end of Gu Shan (Solitary Hill), was one of West Lake's favourite beauty spots. A pavilion called Wang Hu Ting (Pavilion for Viewing the Lake) used to grace the lakeside. In front of the pavilion a terrace was laid out, jutting into the lake. It was a delight to view the scene from here, with serene waters on three sides, rain or shine and particularly during a full-moon autumn night. The plantings of trees and flowers, mainly cassia and maple, added immense beauty to the garden.

At the southwestern end of the West Lake was Hua Gang Guan Yu (Viewing Fish at Hua Gang Pond). Here, in the old days, a small creek flowed from Hua Jia Hill and emptied into the lake. A pavilion was erected on the south side, with a pond in which fishes were raised.

Xiao Ying Zhou is one of the three man-made islets in the outer Lake of the West Lake. Actually, this was an area surrounded by circular embankments. The islet itself is designed in the tradition peculiar to Chinese landscape gardening arts meaning wonderful, superb craftsmanship excelling nature. From south to north, the islets were joined by the nine-bend bridge and adorned with pavilions, terrace halls which overlooked the lake, rockeries and extensive plantings of flowers. These features merged harmoniously with the placid lake water and the surrounding green hills.

Omei Mountain in Szechuan.

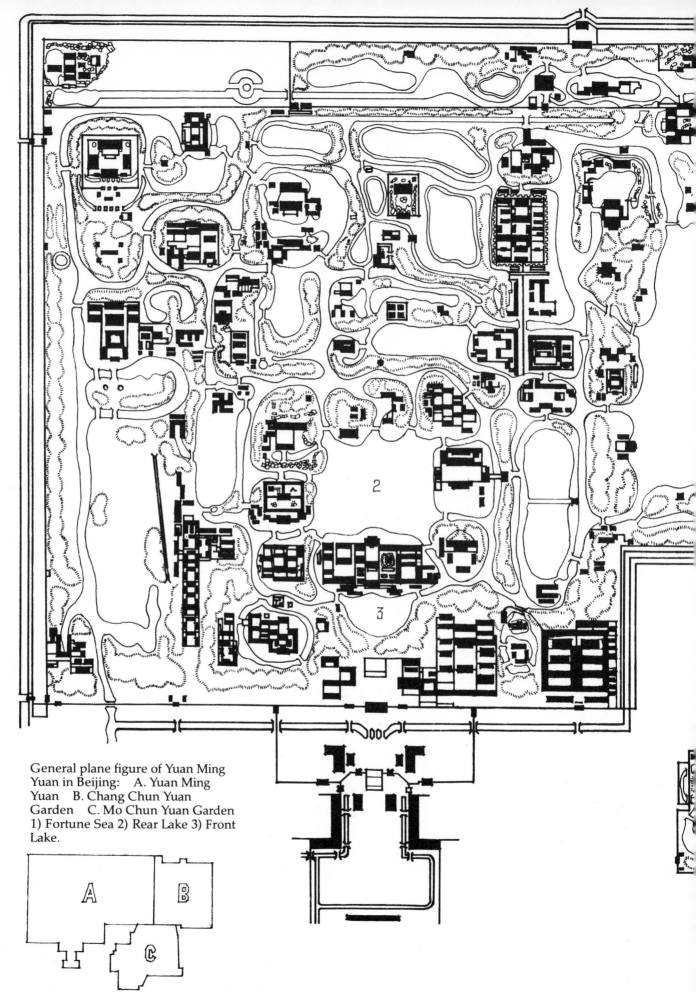

General plane figure of Yuan Ming
Yuan in Beijing: A. Yuan Ming
Yuan   B. Chang Chun Yuan
Garden   C. Mo Chun Yuan Garden
1) Fortune Sea 2) Rear Lake 3) Front
Lake.

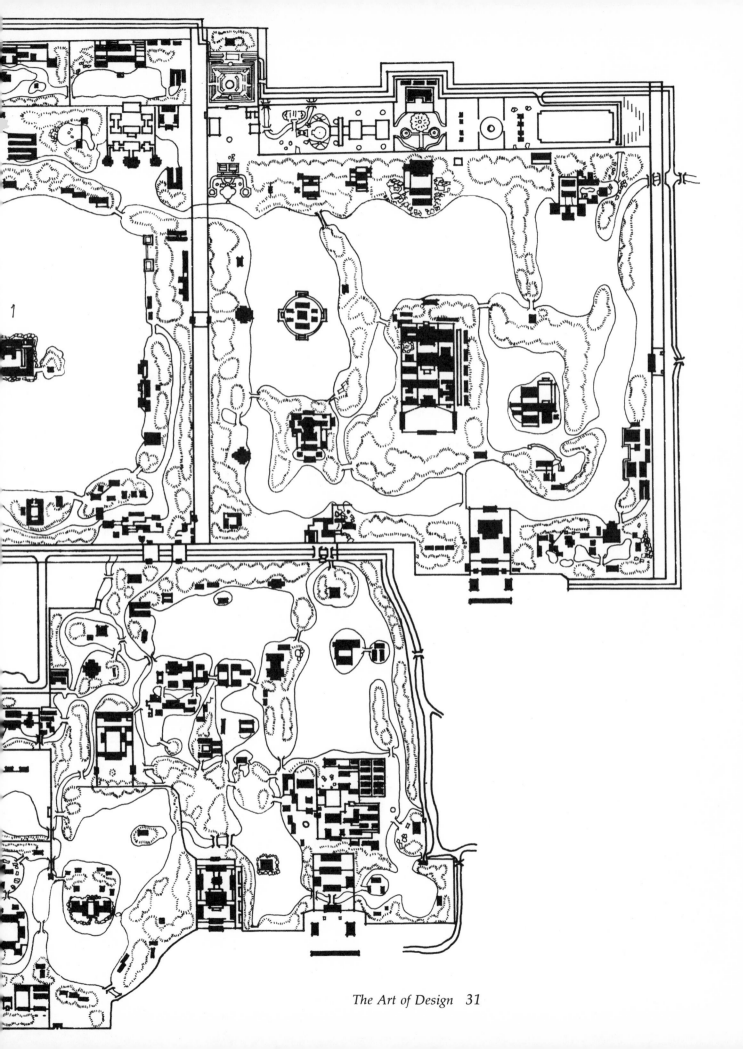

CREATION OF THE ARTISTIC CONCEPTION OF THE GARDEN

Developing the initial artistic conception of a garden is precisely analogous to the creative impulse and vision experienced by poets and artists who sketch out their concepts before they start to flesh out the final form. The mental state necessary to create artistic concepts requires the linking of objective reality with the subjective and emotional results in the reader or viewer which the artist wishes to "elicit".

The response of the viewer which the Chinese landscape architect wishes to evoke is the poetic flavor of the landscape, as do his colleagues in landscape painting. In ancient times, the quality of a garden or garden scene was appraised and criticized by the same standards as those used in literature and art for the same artists, who represented the elite of literature and art, were the leading designers of gardens as well. In the south along the lower reaches of the Yangtse River, the highly regarded garden-designers such as Yu Zhi of the Southern Song Dynasty; Ji Cheng of the Ming Dynasty and Chang Lian, Chang Ran, Li Yu and Chou Hao Da of the Qing Dynasty were recognized as among China's most respected cultural figures. The gardens of Soochow either belonged to scholars and artists or were designed by them. Many of the scholar/artist gardens are extant today and include well-kept residence gardens of Yi Yuan, Wang Shih Yuan and Huan Xiu Shan Zhuang (Mountain Villa) in Soochow. They laid out halls, pavilions, courtyards, rockeries, ponds even a single tree or a single rock in the same manner, with as deep a concern and as profound a creative vision as when they sketched out their paintings in keeping with their personal creative concepts.

The ancient gardening book *Yuan Zhi (Gardening)* written by Ji Cheng (1582 — 1634) remains the best account of the Chinese approach to garden design. The descriptions of nature and the arts of gardening are repeatedly linked with human feeling and interest. The organization and structuring of a garden in space from the total layout to the treatment of individual features in a scene are all conceived in terms of relating to and confirming the viewer's sense of the beauty and metaphysical significance of the natural order. All artistic undertakings must share in the epistemological and esthetical responsibility to raise in the viewer's mind the synchrony of the order of the world and man's proper role in that world. A particularly apt example of the creative demands upon the garden designers is evident in Lui Yuan of Soochow. Here the distinct scenes called Gu Mu Jiao Ke (An Interweaving-branched all Tree), Zhu Jing Xiao Yuan (Small Courtyard of Trailed Bamboos) and Qing Feng Chi Guan (Refreshing Breeze Pond-pavilion) plus the others in the garden exemplify the effects, esthetic and metaphysical, to be realized by the creative use of the formal gardening precepts, changes in size, shape or direction; concrete or abstract relationships; or when viewed as a whole, as an integrated, systematic and rhythmic layout of the natural world, with the scenes sometimes spreading, sometimes contracting. The natural integrity of the garden is sealed by the proper concern for the under-

Beijing opera stage at Ji Xias Shan Zhuang (Whistle Mountain Residence-Garden) of Yangchow.

lying ecological correctness of the plantings.

The Xu Kuo Yuan (Abstractly-wide Garden) in Chang Shu City of Kiangsu Province serves as a classic example of these same principles. It was a waterscape garden which had as its principle organizing structure the wide water surface traversed by the long bend-bridge with pavilions positioned at the center and both ends. This dominant feature related in an esthetically satisfying way the individual features of the garden, including the abstractly-wide placid lake, the buildings and the trees and the flowers along the embankment, in a harmonious and pleasurable waterscape.

THE CREATIVE METHOD

Ji Cheng (1582 – 1634), the famous artist of the Ming Dynasty, was born and raised in the neighborhood of the attractive gardens and grounds surrounding Tai Hu (Grand Lake). During his boyhood, he admired the splendid view of the mountains, waters, trees and flowers surrounding Tai Hu. In his youth he learned landscape painting which was and is traditionally linked with the art of Chinese gardening. He began his professional career in gardening work and finally became a talented and widely respected garden-designer as well as artist. Ji was typical of the host of leading artists who were outstanding garden designers. Such garden-designers/artists include Ni Yun Lin, Chang Nan Yuan, Li Zhu Weng and Zhu Mian. It should be pointed out that all of these artists were especially noteworthy for their skill in the art of planning and executing rockeries. This is not surprising, as the art of rockeries is closely related to the art of painting in that the conceptional sketch-out from the plane surface of the design to the solid embodiment of the completed rockery was based on the principles of painting. In Ji Cheng's book *Yuan Zhi (Gardening)* he carefully explicates the manner in which the art of painting integrates harmoniously with the art of gardening and how the common underlying theoretical principles of esthetics are executed in gardening practice. Ji, like so many Chinese artists, was also a poet. He made his poetry, painting and gardening a three-in-one practice as did both predecessors and successors. His book summarized the developed art of Chinese gardening and the merits of his views are recorded in the classical gardens which he designed.

In his later years he retired to a particularly scenic spot along the middle reaches of the Yangtse River. Here he built a garden near Huai Ning County of Anhwei Province. This site was selected after extensive travel in his earlier years undertaken for the purpose of viewing the beauty of the mountains and waters south and north of his native province to gain insights into the nature of hills, rivers, creeks, rocks and trees, and thereby deepen his impression of them to enlighten his practice of gardening.

Ji Cheng was also an outstanding architect. A substantial section of *Yuan Zhi* is devoted to the design of garden architecture. He suggested that the buildings in a garden should be of a different style than the

Chinese Waters-and-mountains painting.

tidy, square-style of residential buildings then in fashion. He urged that design of a garden be innovative and creative and that the buildings should share these characteristics. As garden-designer/architect he planned and supervised the entire process from design to final construction. From remodelling the existing topography through piling hills and rockeries, digging ponds and lakes, building pavilions and bridges, to the planting of the trees and flowers his hand, eye and mind were omnipresent. The landscape after his rearrangement was invariably more beautiful than it had been before.

Ji Cheng's *Yuan Zhi* is written in ten chapters contained in three volumes. The book starts with site-selection and basic construction layout and concludes with detailed instruction for the fabrication of doors, windows, banisters, etc. The book is in this respect a reflection of the regular process involved in systematically designing and carrying out construction according to the design drawings. But the book is not simply a construction manual, for throughout, it explicates the esthetic principles and creative objectives which must be observed in the making of a beautiful garden.

The creative objectives in designing a garden incorporated in Ji's book fall into five aspects: suitability, taking advantage, refinement, simplicity and changeability or unexpectedness. These five aspects are to be understood in the following way:

Suitability. In Ji's view "the suitability of positioning is of the essence in gardening", meaning that every feature of the garden, whether plant, rock, bridge, tree or building, had a single uniquely suitable position in the garden. Or, as he puts it "to erect a pavilion where it should be erected". He points out that a building in a garden might be sited well and in accord with local conditions, but he goes on to point out that if equal attention has not been paid to the importance of the treatment of details such as a door, a window or a banister, the building loses an element of its harmony with the surrounding scenes.

The word "suitability" must also be understood in the context of the "skillfully appropriate" opening up of a garden path, the siting of trees and flowers, the piling up of hills and rockeries, etc. Suitability must be understood not only in terms of dimensional shapes, positions and directions in space but also in terms of local conditions including not only the changing seasonal qualities of sky, weather and plants but also requirements of the site.

The word "suitability" is also linked with "cause", or objective. No matter whether the garden be big or small, there is one or more objective "causes" or ends served by the garden. For example, a naturally beautiful, significant or striking scene "causes" a garden feature to be placed in a particular position. This sense of suitability implies that there exist in every garden objective ends, or causes, for doing or placing specific things, which are independent of the whim of the designer.

Taking advantage. In *Yuan Zhi* Ji emphasized the necessity or "the skill to get to the cause", that is, to understand and "take advantage of" the scene. There was a couplet written on a scroll in front of the

Cang Lang Ting (Blue Wave Pavilion), a scenic spot in Soochow, which said: "The moon and wind are of no value as they are, yet nearby waters and far-off mountains attract one's feeling." Significant, beautiful scenes exist everywhere: the means of incorporating them in gardening must be based on creative understanding, thought and method.

"Taking advantage" of the surroundings whether nearby or far-off involves every aspect of the site from the simplest to the most profound — the remote peaks, the nearby fields, even the chanting from a nearby Buddhist temple, the song of a fisherman, the flying clouds, the flowing water. Every facet or aspect of the locale could be taken as "advantages" for enriching the scenes in the garden whether they were close at hand, far-off, still or in movement. Further, each scene in a garden must take advantage of every other scene in the garden.

The private gardens of the lower reaches of Yangtse River were rather small in size. It was therefore incumbent on the designer to bring great creative ingenuity to bear so as to provide a wider or more spacious vision within the limited available space. Ji Cheng, whose training and early experience was in this part of China, especially stressed the need to take advantage of everything suitable, whether it was inside, outside, nearby, far-off, in a static state or in movement, as well as the dynamics of the scenes within a garden itself.

In the Yu Yuan of Shanghai there were two Lous (towers), the Wang Jian Lou (Seeing-river Tower) and the Guan Tao Lou (Seeing-waves Tower), placed in high positions, advantageous for viewing the waterscapes on the river outside. Their names succinctly illustrate the reason these two towers were built where they were.

Ji Cheng's talents in classical poetry, art and gardening may be compared to that of a great composer with a deep insight into both Nature and human life and who encapsulates this profoundly felt understanding and love in an everlastingly classical symphony. A classical Chinese landscape garden composed of not just buildings, hills, waters, rockeries, rocks, trees and flowers, but all the nuances incident to its place similarly incorporates a complex of living scenes and landscape scenes not in isolated units but rather in harmony with each other and depending upon and taking advantage of each other.

Refinement. Ji suggested that simplicity, plainness, tranquility, naturalness, gracefulness, elegance, neatness and distinctness were all essential elements which must be incorporated into garden design. In these terms he defined the word "refinement". He concluded his discussion of refinement with the expression "qiu ya qu su". Translated, this means to pursue tastefulness and eschew vulgarity. Here he had reference to such things as painted pillars, carved beams, extravagance and that common form of plagiarism which is epitomized by the faddish pattern, convention or practice.

"Refinement" in Ji's view was only to be achieved by remodelling conventional human styles in accord with the style and features of Nature. He believed that the outcome of building upon natural beauty and the beauty and significance of man-made things accomplished by careful and thoughtful craftmanship could and would even excel nature. He recommended that the garden-site would best be located in or near wooded and hilly areas where the altitude varied and marked differences of topography result in interesting bends, depths, plain and steep places. If such a site is not to be had, then a garden located near a river or lake is a good selection for the natural attractiveness of the dispersed reeds, the dense willows, and all the features with which such spots abound, and it could be markedly enhanced by the artificial refined beauty of buildings, trees and flowers. Ji's thoughtful garden-designs were mainly based on the skilled development of landscapes and waterscapes which appeared to be natural. He admired simplicity, tranquility, refinement and freedom from vulgarity. His poetic, artistic thought and method as applied to the garden represented both the mature statement of the traditional art of Chinese gardening and the codified canon against which subsequent landscapes and waterscapes of China have been judged.

Simplicity. In *Yuan Zhi* Ji emphasized the spirit of simplicity and thrift. Even waste material such as broken tiles and bricks could be used to pave the garden-path and broken ceramic bowls and vases were excellent material to inlay the road-surface. Stone and rock materials which could be readily obtained from nearby mountains, rivers and lakesides cost very little. He said: "Don't consider fetching the so-called rare and wonderful rocks far from the construction site, get them as near as possible. Don't consider the shapes and sizes, broken or intact. The key point is to pile them in hills and rockeries according to sound esthetic concepts to be found in the line drawings of the artists of mountains-and-waters painting. Thus, any stone or rock can appropriately be used to pile up splendid, yet natural, simple, low-cost hills and rockeries." "Tastefulness" and "thrifty" are closely related in Ji's book, for excessive expenditure in constructing a garden commonly leads to vulgarity.

Changeability or unexpectedness. The last of the leading principles governing traditional Chinese garden design is "changeability" or unexpectedness. In Ji's *Yuan Zhi*, achieving the objectives of "contrast and rhythm" in garden construction is to be realized by "adapting to changing circumstances" and "changing circumstances to vary the scenes". In Chinese classical gardens, the range of "changeability" included every aspect of the garden-view, from the design of buildings, to the sum total of all the living or lifeless things of the earth including the moving clouds in the sky, the flowing water in the river, wooded mountains, wind, rain, snow, dew, trees, flowers and herbs, no matter whether they were in static state or in movement — all were to be considered as a dynamic organic whole, changing "with the seasons" and "with the scenes".

eral plane figure of Cang Lang Ting
e-Wave Pavilion) of Zhou Zheng
Garden in Soochow.

In the *Yuan Zhi* there are many ways to infuse "changeability" into the garden as documented by Ji, "changes invoked by chance, concepts, seasons, shapes and physical features of the land". "Changeability" is a subtle creative concept and of particular significance and import in architectural design. Some of the various methods include:

A. In design and construction, all paths, corridors, pond embankments, creeks and bridges should incorporate "suitable" bends, to not only change the scene but also give a sense of extension in space and depth. In so treating waterscapes, bending and winding will render deep and serene waterscenes. Ji said "Where there is a bending and winding flow of waters, there the viewer will sense a deep environment and feeling of nature."

B. The author's preface to *Yuan Zhi* states: "The rising and falling physical features of the site can be used advantageously, build a pavilion on the high, excavate a pond on the low, the surplus earth excavated will be well used to pile hills, thus the physical features of the land are partly reformed in keeping with the desired pattern of the landscape garden." In a smaller garden, remodelling the physical features of the land is particularly necessary to produce a perception of large space in a small area.

C. The "contrast" method often used in Chinese gardening is to contrast the true with the false and the real with the void. The purpose is to make the artificial only perceived as real. Ji contrasted the real mountains and waters which are the artless creations of nature with that of the skillful craftsmanship required to remodel a natural landscape or waterscape, which if suitably done cannot be further beautified.

In Chinese gardens, rockeries are generally called "jia shan" which means artificially-made "false mountains". Two kinds of rockeries are recognized depending upon the material used. One piled up of original rocks quarried from nearby mountains is called "dui jia shan". The other, simply called "jia shan" is made of common stones and rocks found on or in the earth. In both cases, however, the seemingly real mountains were in fact not real, but rather the result of the fine workmanship which makes them closely resemble the real. This form of contrast, if done with impeccable artistry, is considered a major achievement in Chinese gardening.

In the architecture, hills, ponds, trees, and flowers are to be found the sources for creative contrast — not only in gardening but in painting as well.

D. Ji Cheng's theory and method of garden design was posited on the Chinese preference for natural landscape gardening. Ji said: "Architecture, hills, trees, flowers, etc., are better strewn about at random than in a tidy style. The pavilion and terrace oriented to the pond-side and other objects on a horizontal plane must be well-arranged both from the front and behind in keeping with the design, but must appear to be unorganized as in a natural state. Such a layout is much better than a layout of balanced pairs or rows." Ji points out in the "Hill-pile" chapter of *Yuan Zhi* that hills must be piled randomly — some higher, some lower, but all steep and pointed. Tidy and balanced hills present a stiff and rigid appearance just like "a mountain of swords or a row of candles and vases which is not attractive to anybody".

ARTISTIC PRINCIPLES

To build a landscape or waterscape garden of the "wooded, ponded, hilly city-garden" type on a level piece of ground requires a complex and artistic garden design to properly lay out the scenes of hills, waters, trees and flowers, and the garden architectural constructions. In addition, superb craftmanship in the execution of the design is critical if the criteria of suitability, taking advantage, refinement, simplicity and changeability are to be realized. In designing small city gardens, the following artistic principles must be carefully observed:

The Real and the False

In a classical Chinese garden, the layout must be quintessentially appropriate, neither crowded nor scattered, but as in a natural state. Especial attention should be paid to the piling up of hills and rockeries, which if not appropriately designed and built will convey a sense of crowding and disproportion.

The ratio between the ground area and the water surface area obviously influences the entire structure of a garden. Generally, the area devoted to ground planting is relatively larger than that assigned the water area. However, the water feature is always at the center of the landscape design. Once the precisely suitable place for the water feature is established, the pond or bog must be excavated with both an irregular boundary and differing depths. The principle architectural constructions will then be settled near the margin of the pond or radiating away from it. The orientation of the main building whether to the south, east, west or north of the pond will be determined by the direction which affords the finest esthetic view. For example: In two extant Soochow gardens the main garden-construction of Han Bi Shan Fang (Green-jade-like Mountain House) of the Liu Yuan Garden faces northward, while the Lotus Hall of Shi Zi Lin (Lion Grove) faces south toward the lotus pond.

Traditionally, in Chinese gardening the ground or earth means "the true", while "the false" means the water. As a consequence, the appropriate ratio between ground and water is a significant factor in the proper esthetic solution of the real and the false.

Setting off

A traditional Chinese saying is "the red flowers and the green leaves of the peony are both necessary to bring out the best of each". This saying epitomizes the meaning of "setting off". The idea of "setting off" should not be confused with the idea of contrast. Contrast simply points to differences between two or more things. "Setting off", on the other hand, requires both a primary and secondary quality which mutually enhance one another. Setting off is the method of balance in gardening. For example, architectural constructions positioned on one side of a water surface are set off by the rockeries piled up with rocks collected from mountains or lakes, on the opposite side. The manifestly man-made buildings enhance and are enhanced by the natural-looking rockeries. The same effect may be achieved by arranging garden features unevenly in higher or lower positions. An obvious form of setting off is achieved by setting off plants of one colour by plants of another, analogous to the example of the peony plant. Less obvious is the use of "setting off" by planning some garden features so they appear in an open and distinct situation while others are secluded or hidden. These changeable scenes are both thoroughly fascinating and thoroughly characteristic of China's garden practice.

Obviously these practices play an important role in contrast as well as in setting off, but the principle function of the various "setting off" devices is to achieve the objective of changeability.

Assembling and Spreading

"Assembling and spreading" is a very sophisticated principle, and must be understood, in the context of the small city-garden, where the objective of providing many and continually changing scenes demands complex and carefully executed solutions to the esthetic problems involved. The layout of scenes along hills and ponds must be irregular and uneven no matter whether the scenes are big or small. Further, the plantings must not be crowded or scattered.

The object is to assemble the elements of any particular scene so that they have the "solid" appearance of a natural setting, but are sufficiently spread in two senses. First, "solidity" must not be confused with crowding. Natural scenes are never crowded but rather are scattered assemblages of plants. Secondly, scenes must be distinctly delineated so that as the viewer moves from one viewing point to the next he is struck by not only the differences between the scenes but also by the natural "solidity" or "assembling" of each.

By way of explication the following comments may be made: In the Lion Grove of Soochow, though the water surface of the lotus pond is not large, the half circling rockeries around the pond occupy a relatively large area on the east side. From Xiu Zhu Ge (Pruned Bamboo Pavilion) to Liu Jiao Ting (Hexagonal Pavilion), another large area of the pond embankment is comprised of rockeries which makes the lotus pond before the Lotus Pavilion appear too narrow, and the sense of the distance to the rockeries on the opposite shore too short to be pleasing. The stone boat was later added to the pavilion. This addition creates a crowded feeling of the ornamental architecture at a single place on a larger expanse of water. So, the esthetic satisfaction in viewing the Lion Grove is diminished for want of proper attention to the principle of spreading.

In Yangchow, there are several gardens along the Shou Xi Hu (Thin West Lake), which present many scenes made up of piled-up rockeries and man-made hills. The rock-scenes are of two different patterns: the cliff-like and the peak-like. The former is meandering but

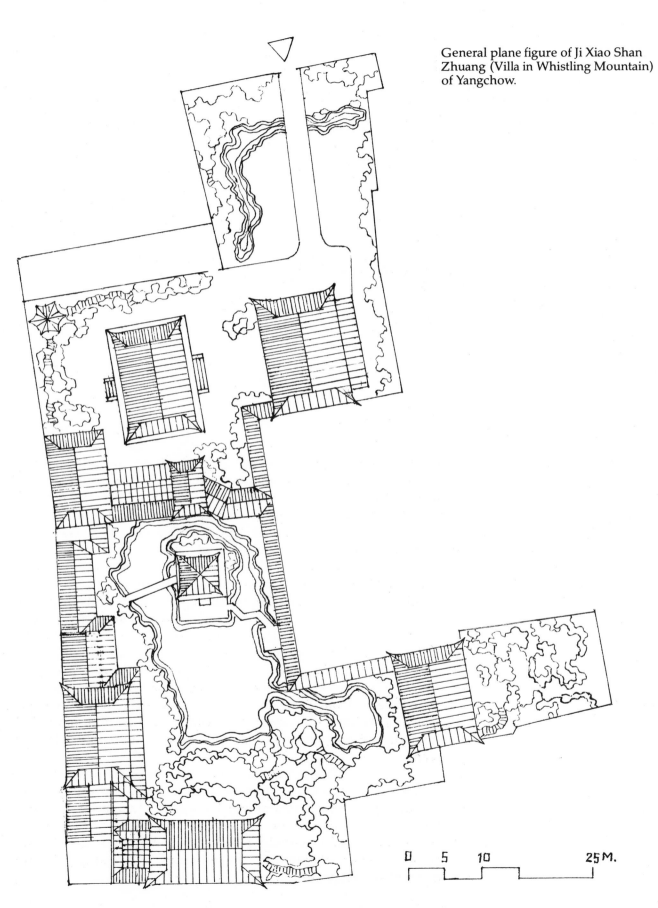

General plane figure of Ji Xiao Shan Zhuang (Villa in Whistling Mountain) of Yangchow.

0 5 10   25 M.

A   B   C

presents a sense of flat groups while the latter are of a winding-type, sometimes combined, sometimes separated from each other. These rock works are very fascinating but lack a solid appearance in their assemblage. So these gardens may be criticized for not observing carefully the attention needed to assemble garden elements in a way to present the viewer with a sense of solidity.

Yet another example will illustrate the virtues of proper attention to and resolution of the principle of assembling and spreading. The residence-garden Ji Xiao Shan Zhuang (Villa in Whistling Mountain) was built with a huge courtyard behind the residence. A covered, double-floored corridor circles the entire garden. The various elements — hills, water and pavilions — can be seen as distinct picturesque scenes of the garden from different levels and viewing places. Further, the skillfully executed windows in floral patterns offer glimpses of the deep layers of plants below. As the garden-design is so compact, the viewer perceives the assembled scenes as solid but natural. In this case the esthetic method of assembling and spreading has been fully realized.

The Huan Xiu Shan Zhuang of Soochow is another example of a well-designed garden in which the assembled scenes are compactly executed but appear natural and satisfying. Though the line leading to the hill is not long, there are multiple scenes of cliffs, caves, creeks, stone houses, and precipices built along the bending, winding path. Although space devoted to the rockeries is not large, the compact, assembled scenes are fascinating.

D

E

Sectional and longitudinal section drawing of Cang Lang Ting in Soochow: A. Ming Dao Tang (Bright Way Hall)   B. Qing Xiang Hall (Delicate Fragrance Hall)   C. Cang Lang Ting (Blue-wave Pavilion)   D. Mian Shui Xuan (Facing-to-water Pavilion)   E. Cang Lang Scenic Lane.

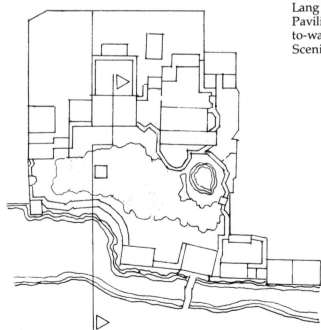

Unevenness and Neatness

In Beijing there is a scenic spot, the Si Yi Xuan (Four Pleasant Season's Open Hall) in the She Ji Tan (Altar to the God of Grains and the Soil). The hall is positioned on the north side of the altar, half built on the ground with the other half built over Yu Dai He (Jade-ribbon River). The hall is designed along tidy, straight lines, enriched with painted banisters, colorful floral leak-walls, red glass windows, and flanked by a long corridor on its east side. East of the corridor are wonderful rockeries irregularly piled up on various levels but notable for their skillful bending, turning and winding line. In this way, a clear-cut contrast is formed between neatness and unevenness in the entire scene. A further contrast is formed by the foundation of the building. Both the part resting on the ground and that over the water were built by laying cut stone plates in tidy and straight tiers. The embankments on both sides are built of various-sized natural rocks. In this way, two different lines are formed. One tidy and the other uneven, yet the contrast results in a quite harmonious feeling.

A private garden, Chang Yuan (Free Garden), in Soochow provides another well-known pattern and clear-cut example of the contrast between unevenness and neatness. The buildings are grouped on the south, west and north sides, connected by a long, bending corridor on the east side. The corridor has a hexagonal pavilion built mid-way. The pond is located in the central area. On the south-east side of the pond the rockeries, consisting of irregularly shaped lake-rocks are piled up in zigzag lines at different levels. The clear-cut contrast between the neat and tidy buildings and the uneven rockeries vividly enriches the pond-scene.

Connecting and separating

In Chinese gardens, piled-up hills and rockeries are a common feature. Trails or paths for viewing not only the scenes on the hills but the gardens below are frequently used. The artificially tortuous mountain trails are paved with stone steps. The trails are designed with many turns, bends and zigzags in keeping with several of the esthetic principles already described. But the interest created by the paths is further enhanced by cut-offs built in the paths forcing the viewer to find some way out. These paths are a readily comprehended use of the principle of connecting and separating.

The same practice is often applied to artificial brooks. On both banks rocks are irregularly scattered in groups, some higher and some lower. The flow of the brook water is cut off at some of these rock groups, so the brook must necessarily become "separated" as it flows under the rocks. For example: In the Yu Yuan of Shanghai, a brook flows through an arch erected mid-way along the front of Laing Yi Xuan (Double-use Veranda). An inverted image of the arch is reflected on the water surface. This reflection not only enriches the scene but also separates the perceived line of the brook by separating the visual flow of the brook. It also breaks the monotonous appearance of the flowing brook continuously extending forward, which makes all brook-scenes look nearly the same.

The Shou Xi He (Thin West Lake) is a placid and clear lake about 4 kilometers long in Yangchow. This zigzag lake was a favorite location to establish lakeside gardens. Downward from Hong Qiao (Rainbow Bridge) a continuous line of gardens extends to Ping Shan Tang (Flat-topped Hill Hall). The gardens contain a wide variety of bridges, towers, pavilions and halls. This well-known scenic area in Yangchow is particularly noteworthy for the many scenes which depend upon the separating and connecting principle to achieve their success.

Cui Hu (Emerald Green Lake) in Kunming, Yunnan Province, is another well-known scenic spot famous for scenes which result from well laid out gardens using the separating and connecting method. The placid lake is separated both in its length and width by several embankments connected by bridges. Towers and ornamental columns erected at the intersections of the embankments both connect and separate the total scene.

Open and close

Man-made caves were also used to create a sense of natural scenes in Chinese gardening. In the Hui Min Yuan of Soochow, a water rockery was built in a cave and stone steps paved on the shallow water level created a pathway through the cave. Fascinating rockery-scenes are faintly seen in the dim light. After traversing several bends and turns through the dark tunnel, the bright exit suddenly appears. This "open and closed" contrast was called "a world of difference" in Chinese gardening.

Level and solid

The proportional relationships between the fluid and the solid, the high and the low, the whole and the part, and between parts has always been emphasized as the means for achieving effective harmony in the layout of Chinese classical gardens. The high rockeries and the level pond-water surface set each other off. On one side, the solid peaks of hills or rockeries and on the other side the clear fluid flow of mountain streams dropping straight downward create a harmony. Or again waterfalls plunging into deep pools, as contrasted with the placid water on the other side of the pond create two unique scenes which bring out the best in each other.

To mold the beauty of nature and the exquisiteness of architecture into a harmonious whole is always the key point in Chinese gardening. Generally, architecture is used as a foil to enrich the natural landscape or waterscape. Architecture, however, is also used to coordinate or take advantage of local topographical features. Ji Cheng observes in his *Yuan Zhi* that "pavilions and terraces stand out unevenly from lakeside or pond, towers appear indistinctly as in rosy clouds". That is to say, skillfully designed architecture pairs with the local landform and the whole of the surrounding environment. Horizontally, bridges, brooks and streams, trees and flowers responded harmoniously with one another: perpendicularly, the mountain ridges and trees work in concert with one another. Artistic effects are produced by up and down, left and right, front and rear, unevenness and neatness, solid and fluid — changeability in layers, colours and shades.

Satisfying garden design is always compact and harmonious: change and difference unify to form lively rhythms. The principle requirement is the proper treatment of the ratio between the whole and the parts and the close and proper relationship between different parts. Good design aims for the coincidence of practical use and sound esthetics.

Ratio and distance of sight

In laying out a garden, the primary ornamental spots are generally established on the opposing sides of hills or rockeries flanking the central feature of a pond or lake. Around the hills and ponds secondary decorative architecture such as pavilions, terraces, corridors and open halls are erected. However, the ratio of distances between primary and secondary ornamental spots and among the decorative spots, must be assiduously and appropriately maintained. The harmony and pleasantness of the garden can only be appreciated if these ratios are observed. The ratio of distance upward, downward or horizontally, no matter whether the ornamental spot is primary or secondary, must coincide with the viewer's field of vision. Otherwise, all elements will lose their lingering charm.

Directional orientation

In traditional Chinese gardening, the directional problem was usually solved by fixing the solids to the north-west and the voids to the south-east. If the pond was located on the north, then the hill or rockery was piled up on the north side of the pond. Thus, the residence building near the waterside faced to the south while the back of the structure overlooking the garden faced north. South-facing buildings were advantageous, as the living quarters were warmed by the sun while the north-facing back and garden were cool during the hot summer.

In the Zhuo Zheng Yuan of Soochow there were two well-known halls, the Datura and the Mandarin Duck. They were built nearly to the high-walled margin of the garden. Two densely-spreading lacebark pines (*Pinus bungeana* Zucc.) were paired evenly to the left and right in the front. In addition, the halls were illumined by blue-glassed windows which extended down to floor level. Thus, they were completely submerged in shade.

On the other hand, the Sui Han Cao Lu (Winter Cottage) in the Liu Yuan of Soochow, facing north, was fenced with stone walls. Evergreen trees such as pines, cypresses, Chinese ilexes and bamboos were planted to form a cool microclimate. On its south side was a lotus pond with several sweet-scented osmanthus and plum trees planted around it. The scene here is bright and sunny.

Exposing and Concealing

Ji Jing (to borrow scenes from nature) was a traditional technique in Chinese classical gardening. Gardens were often established near forests, wooded hills, at river-sides and lake-sides in order to borrow or take advantage of the natural landscape. The layout of gardens obviously varied according to local conditions and the natural surroundings, but usually, the nearby borrowed scenes were exposed while far-off scenes were concealed by walls, houses, trees and rocks. Occasionally, far-off scenes were exposed or concealed depending upon the angle from which they were viewed by interrupting the solid masses by which they were usually hidden.

Line drawing of Qing Xi (Green Brook) of Jian Kang (now Nanking), Southern Song Dynasty (12–13th century).

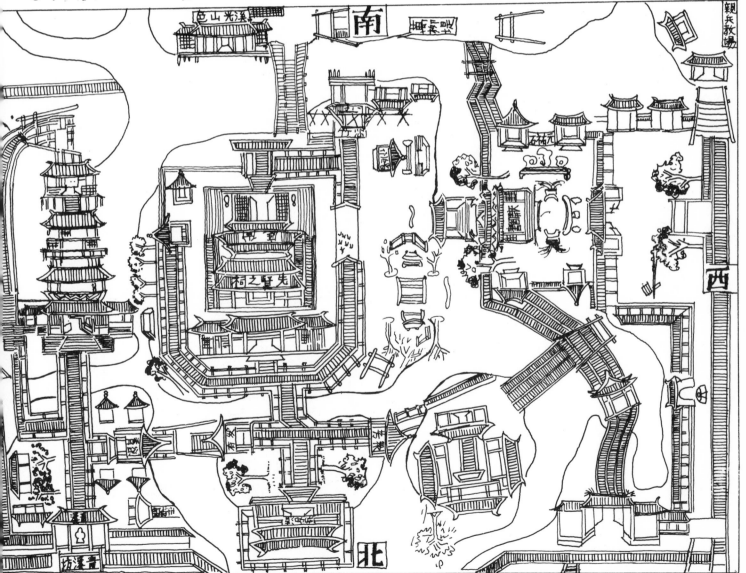

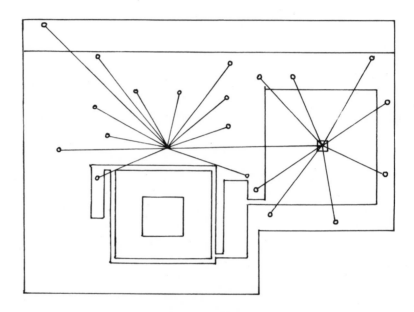

Plane figure of "positive" and "change"
in layout of Yuan Ming Yuan in Beijing.

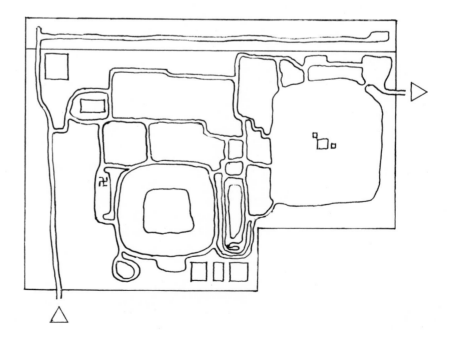

4 Principles of Garden Layout

The Chinese people have been responsive to and deeply involved with the natural order of things throughout the ages. They have endeavored to incarnate it into their cultural life in a variety of ways. That endeavor has been most successful in their gardens. The replication of mountains and waters in a man-made garden was the sublime art of talented gardeners, about whose work Ji Cheng said, "the scenes closely resemble those made by the nature".

The traditional Chinese classical garden usually consists of several scenic sections each done in free style. Each scenic section is unique in shape and content. When looked at as a whole, the garden seems quite complicated but the complexity is much more apparent than real, as the garden is only the systematic layout and correlation of each distinct scene and the appropriate viewing points for each scene.

PRINCIPLES OF LAYOUT

Just as a master drawing measures the success of an artist's creative concept, so a splendid garden measures the success of the Chinese garden designer and builder. The Chinese approach to the arrangement of the garden in space is necessarily based initially on the actual conditions in each distinct area in the garden, whether large or small, upon which a unique scene will be built. Each distinct scenic area is then laid out, together with the points to which the viewer is to be led to view the scene. Lastly, the planner's attention is directed to solving the problem of harmoniously and naturally molding the adjoining limits of each scene so that the overall sense of the garden as well as the distinct scenes conform to the canon of the Chinese landscaping art. The creative concepts embodied in the distinct scenes and their artful integration measures the masterpiece of the Chinese landscape designer.

The traditional rules of layout incorporated in Chinese gardening may be summarized as follows:

A. The garden structure and its appropriate location. Ji Cheng said in *Yuan Zhi*: "In planning the layout of a garden, first of all the gardener must consider all the features of the natural state of the place where the garden will be established." The Chengteh Imperial Mountain Resort may be cited as a fine example of this concept. It is located on mountainous land where the topography is greatly varied and includes upright cliffs, hanging slopes, aged pines, waterfalls, creeks, springs and a patch of plain land. It was upon this plain that a "suitably adapted" group of buildings was placed to both set-off the vivid scenes as well as to provide the view points from which to view the unusual and rugged scenes. The result is considered one of China's most masterful gardens.

B. The relation between layout and scenes. The complexity of the overall garden design and the irregular changes and unexpected variations in individual scenes are closely related. Creative garden scenes are the basic units of the garden and depend upon a correct understanding and use of topographic features to achieve their effect. In turn, the individual scenes, no matter how beautiful and varied, depend chiefly on the creative ingenuity of the talented garden designer to realize and to achieve an integrated total effect. Scenes are not independent units, they are inseparable elements of a garden which in its entirety is a crystallization of the creative concepts underlying the arts of gardening, painting, and architecture.

C. "Borrowing scenes" inside and outside the garden. In *Yuan Zhi* Ji said: "Scenes can be borrowed. In this way the best of each, no matter whether they are a nearby view or a far-off background, inside or outside the garden, can be realized. The key point is the skillful-

Plane figure of Five Aged Pines Garden of Shi Zi Lin (Lion Grove).

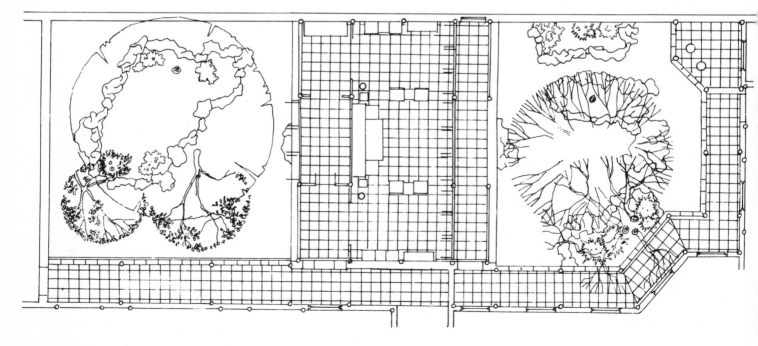

ness in the layout of the inner scenes so that they closely relate to the outer ones. This relationship depends upon and varies with local topographical conditions, the position of pavilions, halls, terraces, rockeries, ponds, bridges, trees and flowers. All of these features must be shown at their best in the integrated layout."

D. Open scenes and closed scenes, diversities integrated into unity. Individual scenes will be different due to microtopographic features and so will change through space, yet they must be linked to each other in an orderly way. In traditional Chinese gardening this order is achieved by the so-called "open scene and closed scene". This means that each scene has a distinct beginning, middle and end. This same device is used in painting a picture. Only by opening and closing each scene separately, and based on microtopographic conditions, can the diverse and varied scenes be integrated into a unified system. Otherwise only disorder and confusion will result.

Sectional and longitudinal section drawing of Gu Wu Song Yuan (Five Aged Pines) of Shi Zi Lin (Lion Grove) in Soochow.

Principles of Garden Layout 51

DIVIDING THE SCENIC AREAS

The layout method used in Chinese garden planning is to first establish the several scenic areas of the garden. This division must proceed in such a way that each scenic area stands out as a prime subject composed of unique features which will convey the sense of a different environment and scenic atmosphere. However, in dividing the garden, all of the separate scenes must be linked in a dynamic fashion into a perfectly organized organic body.

In the traditional landscape or waterscape gardens of China, the prime subjects for different scenic areas generally are mountains, waters, rockeries, paths, trees and flowers. In smaller gardens the prime subjects are trees and flowers, such as groves of bamboos, Chinese sweet gums, osmanthuses, magnolias and lotuses or in waterscape gardens, water courtyards, water corridors, water pavilions, ponds and bridges. In a few gardens, such as the Lion Grove in Soochow, the prime subject of nearly all the scenes is remarkable rockeries.

A good example of a private garden composed of multiple scenic areas is Zhou Zheng Yuan Garden of Soochow. The Yuan Xian Tang (Far-fragrant Hall) is the central scene. On its north side is a waterscape created by the remodelling of a natural scene formed by the Yangtse River. On its south side are precipitous mountain scenes created by man-made rockeries. Its surrounding scenes are made up of the Xian Cang Lang (Small Blue-wave) water courtyard, the Loquat Garden with its showy green leaves and golden fruits, and the Hai Tang Chun Wu (Begonia Flower-bed of Spring).

The perception of the limitation of space available for a garden can be overcome to a certain extent by the division into scenic areas. The perception of a larger space results from the diversity and changes experienced as the viewer moves from one scenic area to the next. The Summer Palace in Beijing presents a typical pattern. Space in the garden seems unlimited due to the division into distinct scenic areas each giving a sense of a different environment, atmosphere and unique features. When the visitor enters this palace-garden, the vast expanse of the water surface in the Qian Hu (Front Lake), undulating with blue waves in the shining, sunny open air, gives him an impression of vastness in space. As the visitor moves on to the scene in Hou Hu (Rear Lake) he is struck by the quite different scene resulting from the vertical movement of the hills and mountains which convey a sense of unlimited vertical space. Following the winding path in the dense shade of the weeping willows on both sides he is brought to the secluded ravines where thriving, colourful flowers in a sea of green plants appear. From this location, the magnificent architectural group on Longevity Hill greatly enriches the mountainous landscapes on the height. On reaching the top of Longevity Hill, the scenes both nearby and far-off are in sight on every side. The major separate garden scenes are further enriched by a number of smaller scenic spots contained within them, each of which has its own features. Some of the garden scenes are designed to represent scenic spots in other parts

Middle part of
Zhou Zheng
Yuan Garden.

of China, so a visit to the Summer Palace will acquaint the visitor
with scenes from other places.

The scenic features of each scenic area must be clearly delineated as
between their primary and secondary position to avoid the appearance of an even and, hence, bland distribution. The common practice
in Chinese gardening is to lay out one scenic area as the principle
scene and treat the other smaller ones as its satellites. Thus, excellent
contrast between them will result. The scenic areas are positioned so
that larger or smaller areas, dense or sparse plantings, etc. are inter-
spaced to produce a rhythmic change in scenes. Frequently rockeries
or small courtyards are used to separate scenes and help provide a
sense of rhythmic change. After passing through several such inter-
spaced areas via a winding route the visitor finally enters the primary
scenic area. This is called the "implicit" or "veiled method of inter-
space" in Chinese gardening.

The common means of dividing scenic areas depends upon the use
of walls, opened windows, pavilion-corridors, halls, rockeries, and
small satellite scenes of trees and flowers. The enclosing walls are
usually low, with bypass corridors and opened windows, often partly
shaded by rockeries, trees and flowers, to avoid monotony and stiff-
ness.

Perspective view of small rock-courtyard of Liu Yuan Garden in Soochow.

The scenic areas in smaller gardens are connected by paths or other guide lines designed both to bring attention to scenes along the way and to lead to the different scenic spots. In larger gardens, scenic areas are divided according to direction. Thus, the Liu Yuan Garden is structured on the east, middle and west three areas, while the Zhou Zheng Yuan Garden is divided into the east and west parts. It should be reiterated that there are gardens within gardens in these large scenic areas. In smaller gardens, ponds are usually used as the prime subject of scenes. Surrounding the water area rockeries, pavilions, halls, trees and flowers are laid out. As the pond is the primary center of the garden, the paths or guidelines usually wind around it through the secondary scenes.

These divisions of the garden space vary by size, depth, height, length, degree of brightness, openness and shade. All these divisions in space are organized into an integrated spatial system emphasizing rhythmic harmony and vivid contrast to serve as foils for observing features of the garden.

THE METHODS OF SCENERY-LAYOUT

In traditional Chinese gardening, there are several methods employed to lay out scenes including: scenes to be separated, by contrast, by matching, by "borrowing", and by framing.

In Classical Chinese gardening, the division into scenic areas is usually called **scenes to be separated** or blocked up. This method in practice means that two scenic spots of different features are separated by a boundary of water in cases where a sense of horizontal expanse is desired or by an undulating earth berm, 3 — 4 meters high, set so as to block the horizontal line of sight. Other methods of blocking or separating include the use of stands of trees, hedgerows, white wall with exits or windows to reveal outside scenes, open corridors, wall-sided corridors, double-story corridors, etc. These separations sometimes become the backgrounds of the divided scenic areas or even the subject of the area.

Walls are solid boundaries which cut off the adjacent scenic areas, while tree-stands and open or windowed halls are semi-blocking boundaries through which the adjoining scenes are faintly visible. Thus, when the visitor enters such a hall he will get a first impression of being in a well-landscaped place where there are mountains, waters and forests.

The entrance of the Liu Yuan Garden was exquisitely designed around a group of gated, covered corridors, and different sized halls connected by passageways. Looking through the ornamentally designed windows, the viewer first sees several small stands of green bamboos (Bambusa textllis McCl.). The quiet atmosphere established on entry is gradually changed as he passes through two small courtyards with dappled light and shade, then finally emerges in the bright primary scenic area of the garden.

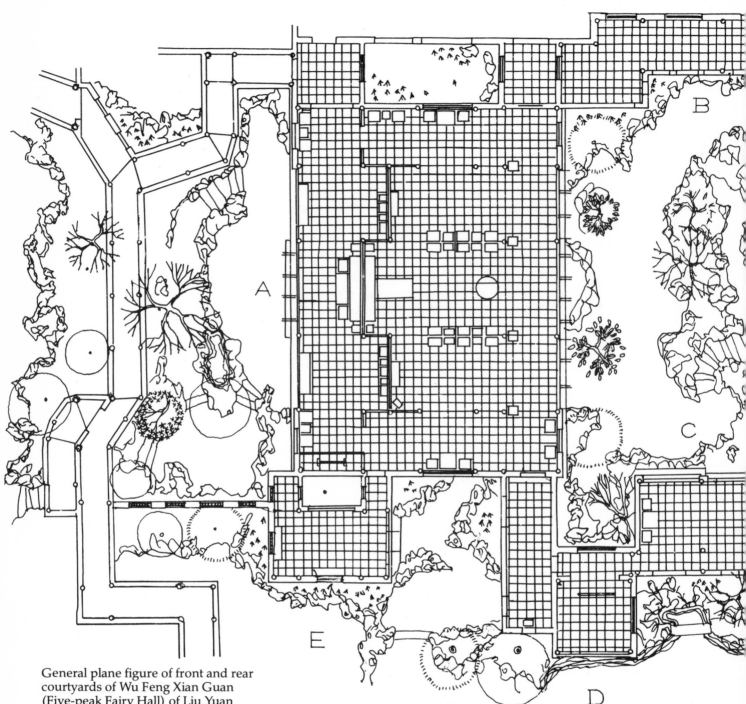

General plane figure of front and rear courtyards of Wu Feng Xian Guan (Five-peak Fairy Hall) of Liu Yuan Garden in Soochow: A. Five-peak Fairy Hall B. Crane's Dwelling Place C. West Storey D. Breeze Pond-hall E. place of an ancient well.

Most private gardens are obviously constructed within a limited range of space. The garden designers brought all their skills to bear to give a feeling of a wider and higher space. The traditional methods depend upon building small and exquisite architectural constructions of rockeries, pavilions, terraces and halls on different levels to increase the perception of vertical space. To lend a sense of horizontal spaciousness, trees and flowers are planted in patterns of light and shade; ponds with irregular embankments are dug, crossed by bend-bridges; and scenic areas are connected by bending, zigzag, winding paths. These devices are also used in landscape painting to draw out an unlimited view from a small scene.

Sectional and longitudinal section drawing of Wu Feng Xian Guan (Five-peak Fairy Hall) viewing from east in Liu Yuan Garden of Soochow.

In the Zhou Zheng Yuan Garden of Soochow, one small water-scape, in the middle scenic area, is designed in such a way as to seem much larger and deeper. The water surface between the east and west embankments is very narrow, but the stone beam-bridge is built in a zigzag fashion which not only lengthens the bridge but also the linear perception of the pond. On the east end, weeping willows are planted along the waterside against a green hill background. Aged elms grow along the west bank, backed by an exquisite group of buildings. The water surface divided by the bridge from south to north and the waterside pavilion Xiao Cang Lang (Small Blue-wave) on the south, built over the watery surface supported by pillars which leave a space underneath, lead the line of sight to the reflection of the images of He Fang Shi Mian Ting (All-sides Lotus Pavilion) and Xiang Zhou (Fragrant Islet) from the opposite bank and divide the pond on the east-west axis. The end result of this immensely creative layout is to widen the viewers perception in all directions. On the north bank of the pond are a group of miniature scenic spots laid out beside a bend-corridor. Through open air windows pierced in the corridor walls the viewer faintly sees other pavilions, halls, rocks, trees and water scenes so the confined space is perceived as being open and broad on all sides. This is a splendid example of a layout used to create a visual perception of extension in a small place.

Principles of Garden Layout 57

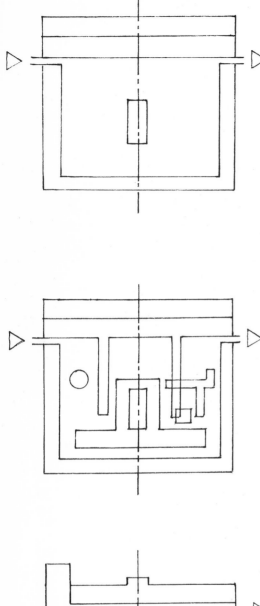

Plane figure of "positive" and "change" in layout of Chang Chun Yuan Garden.

By contrast is another important layout method used in classical Chinese gardening. To bring out and highlight the differing characteristics of the elements in a scene requires creating contrasts in manifold and ever-changing ways: brightness against shade, perpendicular against horizontal, high against low, the big against the small, spreading against merging, movement against quiet and the contrast between colours. These contrasts are realized in a variety of ways: out of a long, densely shaded path through willows a bright flowerbed appears; under precipitous-looking rockeries lays a placid pond; a few wonderful rocks scattered under an aged huge pine; creek water flows through broad and narrow waterways; in a quiet courtyard the murmuring sound of a stream breaks the stillness; in an all-green stand of trees a red pavilion is placed. In the larger Soochow gardens like Zhou Zheng Yuan Garden, Liu Yuan Garden, Cang Lang Ting Garden and Shi Zi Lin (Lion Grove Garden), there were tens of big or small spatial areas to lay out.

Rockeries and ponds were generally established as the primary focus of the garden in the South, while architectural features not badly needed in the warm climate were few and scattered. The Southern gardens depended principally on contrasts between plant materials, dense or scattered, sunny or shady. On the other hand, contrast between tidy architectural constructions and natural scenes epitomized the gardening style in North China. The many buildings required had to be carefully integrated into the total garden design to protect the occupants. For example: the Chengteh Mountain Resort in Jehol Province consists of a group of tidy architectural constructions which contrast with wild mountain scenes. Its entrance is formed by a central group of palaces flanked by other buildings symmetrically oriented along two parallel axes. A visitor enters through the entrance hall, goes through a series of orderly indoor and outdoor areas, and finally reaches the Tien Shan Historical Sites where the contrast provided by the wild mountain scenes in the distance result in a thoroughly satisfying esthetic experience. Yet another example is the Jing Xin Zhai Courtyard in the North Sea Garden in Beijing. The entrance and passage corridor were laid out in a tidy rectangular form with a placid pond in the middle. To provide contrast, the other courtyards were built in an irregular free style of various shapes to provide contrast in architectural construction.

Contrast between the bright out-of-doors and the shady enclosure is successfully used in the layout of the courtyard in front of the Sui Chu Hall and the back courtyard of the Imperial flower garden of the Summer Palace in Beijing. The front courtyard is a horizontal plane court fully exposed on all sides while the back courtyard is enclosed by exquisite rockeries of varying heights.

By matching is another of the traditional methods of layout used in Chinese classical gardening. Just as the layout on a horizontal plane is designed to make scenic spots unique and varied, so the scenes viewed through patterned glassless windows or gateless exits in the walls of corridors or halls were often placed to match two

Sitting kiosk

Color illustrations photographed in South China Botanical Garden, Canton, by the author.

A corner of Palm Garden

Arecastrum romanzoffianum

Plate 1

Waterside pavilion

Waterside garden scene

Reflecting scenery in water

Plate 2

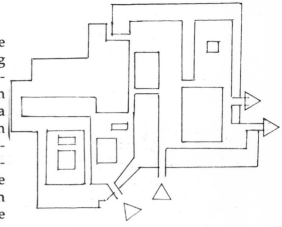

scenes viewed through two such openings. The matched scenes were usually composed to be seen through passageways or from a resting place but were sometimes located in the open. Under any circumstance, the two scenes seen must be related to one another in some significant way. Thus a far-off scene might be matched with a small, delicate closeup scene. Or a natural scene matched with an architectural scene. Scenes viewed through glassless windows or gateless exits are just like pictures in picture frames — the viewer's attention is focused on the picture or scene. Matched scenes must be unique and varied, but related. So wooded hills are matched with architectural constructions; one side of a pond matched with the other; trees matched with flowers; rockeries matched with waters, etc.

Matched scenes are often seen in the classical gardens of Soochow. In the Zhou Zheng Yuan Garden, looking from the Loquat Garden through the flank wall exit, the Xiang Xue Yun Wei Ting (Fragrant Snow and Colourful Cloud Pavilion) appears like a fascinating picture mounted in the frame in the wall matched by Shan Ting (Fan-shaped Pavilion) on the West Side. In the Yi Yuan Garden, a big mirror in the Mirror Pavilion beautifully reflects the picturesque Spiral-shell Pavilion on the rockery on the opposite side matched by a pond scene.

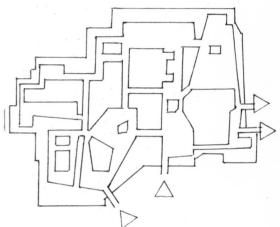

By borrowing as stated in the famous gardening book *Yuan Zhi,* written by the talented artist and garden-designer Ji Cheng, "to borrow scenes is significant in gardening. Borrow the best nearby or far-off, inside or outside the garden, the scene will be much enriched." The scenes to borrow vary with the seasons of the year and viewing angles. Planting trees or building an architectural feature to conceal objects not required to make a scene are advisable.

In the Chengteh Mountain Resort of Jehol, the viewer sees the far-off precipitous Seng Mao Feng (Monkhat Peak) and Luohan Feng (Arhat Peak) as if they were inside the resort. This skillfully borrowed scene mingles with the scenes inside. However, the enclosing wall underneath the hillside was kept out of sight. Thus, the natural far-off scene and the man-made scenes on the hill were integrated into a picturesque landscape.

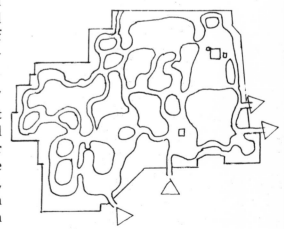

By framing is also called the "Technique of Picture Composition" in Chinese Classical gardening. As scenes outside the garden are not always worthy to be included, it is necessary to select one or two and make pictures of them by using frames of pavilion columns, corridor windows and wall exits to focus the picturesque outer scenes and hide what is not required. For example: in the Summer Palace of Beijing, there is a beautifully framed picture of a pagoda on Yu Quan Shan (Jade-spring Hill) created by the pavilion columns of Hu Shan Zhen Yi Ting (Genuine Lake-hill Pavilion). Framed window scenes in series are commonly used to add depth and dimension to small garden scenes. This is done by constructing a passageway along or around the scene. In the walls of the passageway a succession of window or wall exits are cut. Thus many courtyard scenes are created by the "techniques of picture composition".

Plane figure of "positive" and "change" in layout of Qi Chun Yuan Garden; the lengthwise rectangle-shape is the principal structure.

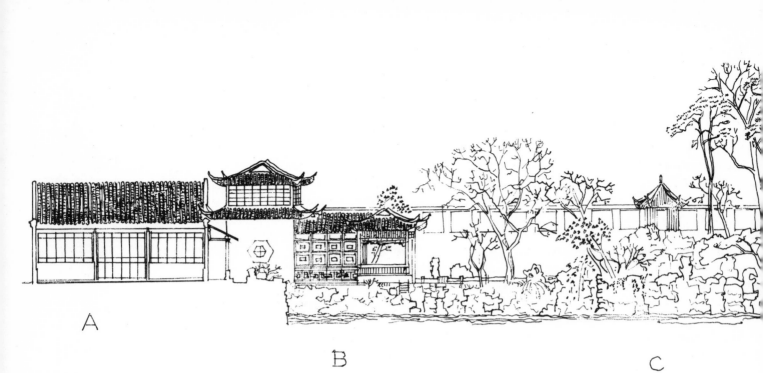

Sectional and longitudinal section drawing of an architectural group in Yi Yuan Garden of Soochow: A. Zhan Lou Tang (Exquisite Show-hall)   B. Hua Feng Zhai (Painted Boat-room)   C. Luo Ji Ting (Spiral Pavilion)   D. Xiao Cong Long (Little Blue-wave Pavilion)   E. Jin Li Ting (Golden Chestnut Hall)   F. Xian Qin Guan (Fairy Musical Instrument Hall)   G. Ou Xiang Xie (Fragrant Lotus-root Pavilion).

E   F   I-I

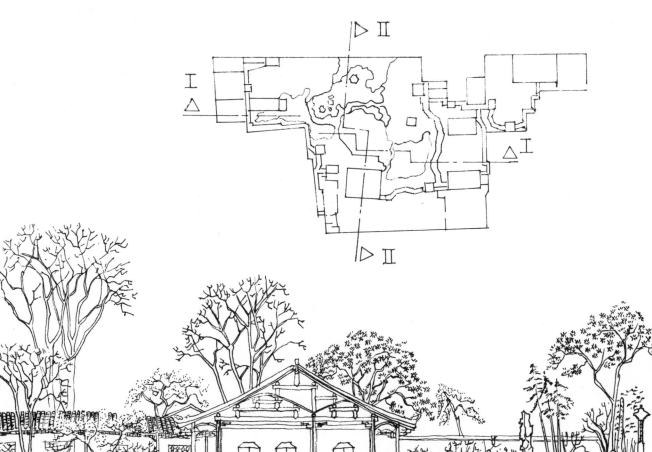

G   II-II

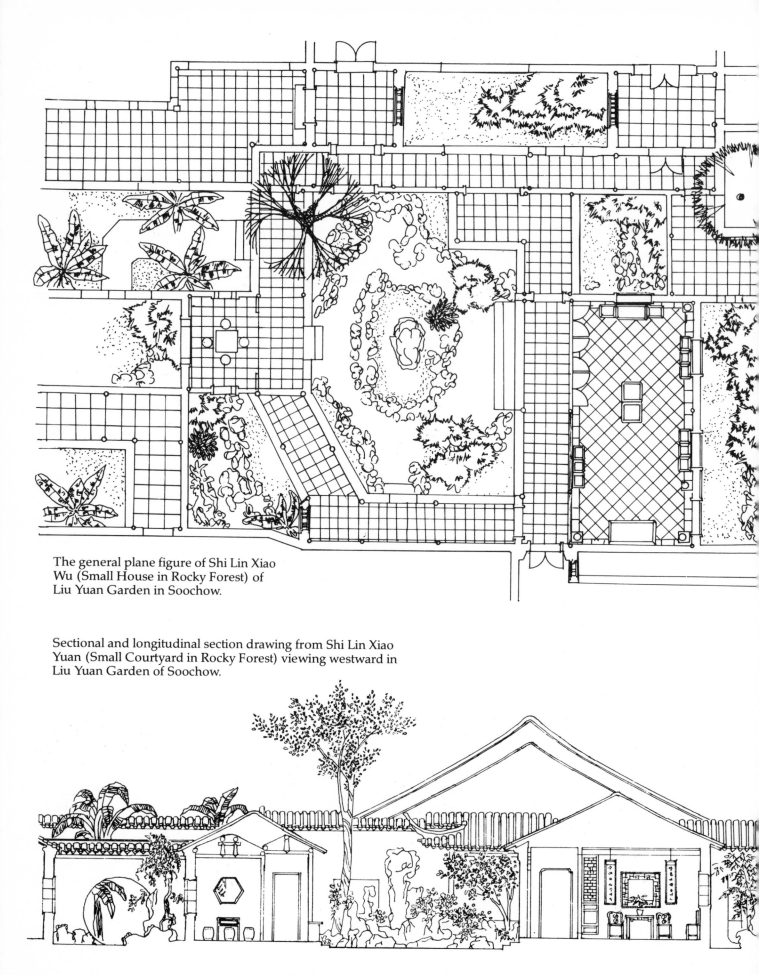

The general plane figure of Shi Lin Xiao Wu (Small House in Rocky Forest) of Liu Yuan Garden in Soochow.

Sectional and longitudinal section drawing from Shi Lin Xiao Yuan (Small Courtyard in Rocky Forest) viewing westward in Liu Yuan Garden of Soochow.

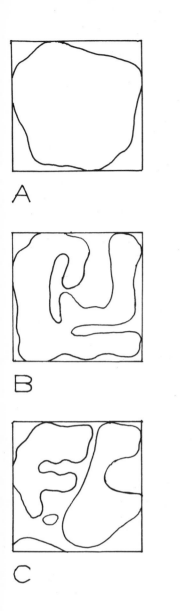

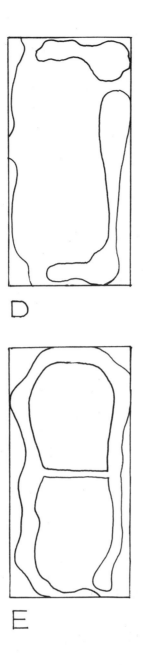

Plane figure of fundamental patterns laid out in Qi Chun Yuan (Beautiful Spring Garden) in Yuan Ming Yuan of Beijing: A, B, D, E, F, (Yuan Ming Yuan) and C (Qi Chun Yuan Garden).

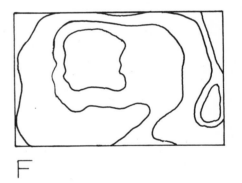

The Layout pattern of the Yuan Ming Yuan Garden analysed

Yuan Ming Yuan Garden in Beijing may be taken as a typical pattern to show the structure of a palace garden consisting of architecture, hills, water, rocks, trees and flowers. This famous garden (which was totally destroyed in the aggressive war staged by the British-French Allied Forces in 1860) was laid out on a structure formed by three main gardens: the Yuan Ming Yuan (The North-west Plateau Garden), Chang Chun Yuan (The Great Plains of China), and Qi Chun Yuan (The Coastal Area of South-east China) gardens.

The whole garden was designed to symbolize the topography of China, that is, the Great Plain of North China, the Great Plateau of North-west China and the coastal area of South-east China. These three areas are the three main elements of the garden. From this north-west to east axis the secondary and satellites scenes spread out radically. The separate scenic areas are divided by water courses and connected by bridges.

Yuan Ming Yuan Garden was built on level ground but had rich resources of water that were used to great advantage by the garden designers to lay out the general plan of the garden. At its north-west corner behind the Purple-Green Mountain Villa a rockery named Han Shan (Cold Hill) was piled up to an extraordinarily high level to symbolize the Kunlun Mountains on the plateau of North-west China.

The Fu Hai (Good Fortune Sea), about one-half a square kilometer in size, was located on the east of the garden to symbolize the East Sea of China. The three islets: Peng Lai, Mo Zhang and Ying Chow were copied from Hu Xin Dao (Lake-islets) in the West Lake of Hangchow. The Fu Hai was square-shaped along the central axis with two related rectangular water surfaces extending perpendicular to the main axis.

The Chun Hua Pavilion was constructed in the center of the level area symbolizing the Great Plain of China. In this area the scenic spots were greatly varied. These two gardens (Yuan Ming Yuan and Chang Ching Yuan) were designed along lines similar to the gardens of the West in that they were of a geometric style and laid out symmetrically under the supervision of the Italian missionary and painter then working at the Qing court during the reign of Emperor Qian Long (1736 — 1796). At the northern end of Chang Ching Yuan (Forever Spring Garden) behind the Ze Lan Tang (Purple-blue Hall) a set of European palaces in Baroque and Rococo styles were set. The design of these halls and associated constructions were carried out by two Frenchmen, P. Micheal Benoist and Jean Deni Attiret.

The Qi Chun Yuan Garden was originally several, independent small gardens which were integrated into a unified garden after the reconstruction of the garden in the years 1723 — 1735. On the irregular square-shaped area, four long, rectangular water surfaces and two broad water surfaces were used to build up the waterscapes. The land and water scenes were irregularly divided in a manner similar to that seen in nature. This garden used the traditional Chinese style of landscape design and so differed from the garden styles of the West used in the other two sections of the garden.

Scenes in Zhou Zheng Yuan
Garden, Soochow.

North water-courtyard of Xiao Cang Lang (Small Blue Wave) of Zhou Zheng Yuan Garden, Soochow.

Xiang Zhou (Fragrance Islet) of Zhou Zheng Yuan Garden.

Rock-wall and cave entrance of Huan Zhu Zhung (Beautiful Surrounding Mountain Villa), Soochow.

The rockery of Cang Lang Ting (Blue Wave Pavilion), Zhou Zheng Yuan Garden.

5 *Piling-Up Hills and Rockeries*

In Chinese gardening history, the piling-up of hills and rockeries occurred very early, beginning with the imperial palace-gardens of the Qin (221 − 207 B.C.) and Han (206 B.C. − A.D. 7) Dynasties. Through ages of development and improvement of this art, it became one of the unique features in Chinese classical gardens. The canons of traditional Chinese abstract landscape painting greatly influenced the formalization for building up hills and rockeries in Chinese classical gardens. Throughout China's long history Chinese gardening and landscape painting were closely related. Generally, the man-made hills or rockeries were called "false mountains". Ji Cheng said in his famous gardening book *Yuan Zhi*, "to pile-up false mountains correctly, they must be made to look real and natural — they are miniature mountains modelled after nature by the arts of gardening".

The mountains are still and quiet while waters are lively and full of movement, so beautiful scenes must be formed by the joining both of them in good garden design. Mountains without plants present a bare and forbidding appearance. Natural landscapes are composed through the harmonious blending of mountains, waters and plants. Chinese landscape gardening was based on these three elements all remodelled and reorganized in the spirit of the nature of things and the canon of natural beauty.

The mountains are formed by nature in a variety of figures, structured of rocks and earth. They vary in figure from one topography to another area. They present fantastic scenes in one place and attractive scenes in another. Mountains stand alone or in groups, they present a variety of shapes, no two the same. Precipitous peaks reach to the sky, undulating ranges flow easily between plains, gently sloping hills dot every natural landscape, all are marked by unique slopes, dimensions, groupings, materials and configurations.

In Chinese gardening, a man-made hill or rockery, if standing alone, is designed so that the distance from the foot to the midpoint rises gradually, repeating the natural pattern of single mountains surrounded by rock falls which form the foothill. Beyond the midpoint the "false mountain" might be piled in any one of a number of ways in accord with the local topographical conditions and the surrounding landscapes. Thus, if the garden was situated in a hilly area the top half was gently sloped and rounded. If, on the other hand, the surrounding natural landscape was made up of precipitous mountains the top half is built up of angular rocks to harmonize with the borrowed view. In the case of a multiple summit "false mountain" the sloping lower section extended beyond the midpoint in keeping with the outlines on foothills naturally found surrounding mountain ranges. Naturally the vegetation on the sunny side of the hill is sparser than on the shady side as the soil of the latter is moister than the former. Plants are situated on the hills carefully and according to their preferred habitats.

In making a hill or rockery, rough sketches detailing not only the elevations from several sides but a plane view, looking down on the formation, were first drawn. In this way the size, height, position and background were visualized so all the design objectives sought in the garden were correctly realized in a naturally harmonious and esthetical way. The position, size, figure, etc., of man-made hills or rockeries must be varied in keeping with the objectives of the garden. If the garden is designed to replicate mountain scenes, the rockeries and hills must be large and centered in accord with the topography of the site groups. If, on the other hand, the garden is a waterscape, the rockeries must be smaller and should be scattered to beautify the central scene.

TYPES OF HILL AND ROCKERY GARDENS

Big-Hill Gardens

Big, wooded hills are often positioned as the central focus in a garden. Pavilions or halls are built on or near the top so the viewer can overlook the surrounding scenes both near and far-off. The objective in these gardens is to create a wide perception in space. Such big hills are constructed principally of earth. Wonderful rocks were carefully chosen to decorate both the hill and the trails along which they were scattered to help create and define the varying scenes. Occasionally a rockery built entirely of rock was interpolated but only as one scene among many. Because the main objective to be served by the big-hill garden was to instill the perception of an extensive verdure-covered expanse viewed from a height, earth was needed to support the dense plantings of trees and shrubs.

Medium-Hill Gardens

Medium-sized hills were often piled at the center position in the gardens along the lower reaches of the Yangtse River and other gardens of the South. Such hills are often seen in the layout of private residence-gardens. Generally, earth is piled up first to shape the mountain. Then the rocks of various shapes are added and fixed as an outer layer to form a natural-looking rocky mountain with cliffs, peaks and caves. The esthetic objective of such gardens is to replicate the natural feature and topography of the south of China.

Small Rockery Gardens

The space available for the most private residence-gardens was rather limited, yet rockeries proportional to the available space can be laid out, if skillfully designed and constructed. In Chinese gardening, such small scale rockeries were traditionally called "Essays of Rockeries", meaning that rockeries of small size were analogous to that widely admired form of literature, the essay, which dealt cogently and succinctly with a topic in limited space.

Examples of Small Rockery Gardens

The Ge Yuan (Specific Garden) is representative of the art of small rockeries in Chinese classical gardening. It is notable for being closely related to the Yangchow School of Landscape Painting. The mountain scenes of Qiu Shan (Autumn Mountain) in the Ge Yuan Garden closely resembles those of real mountains. The viewer climbs stone steps carrying him up the rough and rugged path. At every turn a new view unfolds before him — at one moment a scene of open sky appears, next a cave, then yawning ravines upon reaching the top of towering cliffs. All of these scenes are clothed in a series of carefully selected and cunningly designed plantings. Qiu Shan offers a breathtaking view of the varied scenes through which the viewer has passed and a staggering sense of the extraordinary coherence and integration of the total garden design.

The rockeries and pond of the Lion Grove in Soochow are widely renowned as one of the outstanding scenic spots of the garden. In front of the pavilion and hall made of colored tile roofs with upturned eaves and red columns, a dazzling but harmonious landscape of miniature mountains-and-waters was carefully laid out.

The Guan Yuan Fang (Cloud-crowned Peak) in the Liu Yuan Garden located in Soochow is a single rockery erected in the center of a courtyard. Though small it is wonderfully shaped. Its skillful shaping and positioning make it one of the most inspired and dramatic examples of Chinese landscaping. Several rocks, together with trees and numerous flowering plants in pots skillfully scattered around the mountain, create one of those beautiful scenes which was and is traditionally sought in the design of residence gardens.

THE MAIN POINTS OF CREATIVE WORK

In the composing and shaping of a "false mountain" no matter whether complicated or simple, the principal structural features and intention must be immediately obvious. Otherwise, it will be perceptually vague and look untidy. In laying out a rockery it is important

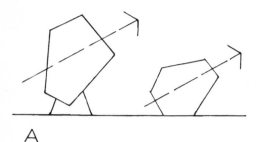

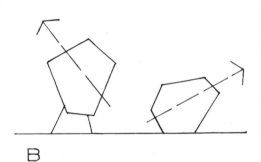

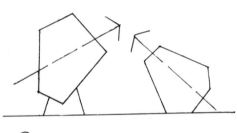

Sketch map of scenic rocks
harmoniously concerted:
A. postures unanimously in same
direction (no good)
B. postures in opposite direction (no
good)
C. postures matched in face-to-face
direction (good).

to differentiate between what is primary and what is secondary. Therefore, suitable and distinct contrasts of the various features of the mountain is important. Rockeries must be the reduced but lively epitomes of the real mountains found in nature.

Levels, Rise and Fall

Both single mountains and a group of mountains, must be constructed to present different levels both from front to back and in elevation from the gentle mountain foot to precipitous peaks. Obviously the rise and fall of a single mountain must be different in range and size from a group of mountains, the latter being not only higher but also of greater areal extent.

Look around and echo

In laying out a group of mountains, the ridges and peaks must be designed to "echo" each other over a distance and between primary and secondary mountain ranges. This obviously means that dimensions, shapes and orientation must be organized in a fashion to present the perception of similitude. Further, the viewer's eye must from every viewing point be led to "look around", back and forth and up and down. Rock scenes will be judged ideal when their shapes, orientation and dimensions are layed out harmoniously and fit together as in nature.

Tortuous, Convex and Concave Features

The circumferential line of the foothills from which the ascending mountain arises (usually about the midpoint) must be tortuous and winding in keeping with the rising and falling line of the foothill levels. This is to say that the upper foothill line which marks the change of slope between the gently rising foothills and the steep mountain top must not be constructed at a constant level but must rise and fall in a dramatic way. Moreover, in piling up the upper part of the rockery, concavities and convexities must be incorporated in the face of the mountain to provide cliffs, caves and mountain tongues just as lines and folds are used in a landscape painting. Such concavities and convexities not only enhance the viewer's perception of the natural quality of the mountains but will provide a sense of mystery and infinity.

Harmony and Proportion

In the piling-up of hills and rockeries careful attention must be paid to maintaining both the harmony and balanced proportion of the primary features of the mountains. Thus, size and elevation, openness and construction, rise and fall must be conceived as a unified whole. Yet, asymmetrical features must be incorporated to enrich the sense of rhythmic change and to avoid monotony and a feeling of sterility.

THE USE OF MOUNTAINS-AND-WATER PAINTING FOR REFERENCE

In the piling-up of hills and rockeries, the Chinese garden artists kept in the forefront of their mind the concepts embodied in water and mountain paintings. Landscape painting had long been the most highly regarded form of painting. From the reign of emperor Huizong in the Song Dynasty, himself an accomplished painter, close attention was paid by artists to the thoughtful rendering of natural landscapes both in their outward and visible form and in their inward and spiritual significance. Many artists from this period onwards chose to convey their vision of the natural and proper order of things not only in painting but also in the design and layout of gardens which gave a more immediate expression of these principles. So landscape artists were frequently also landscape architects and a common perception of the natural order is to be found in paintings and gardens.

In both Chinese landscaping and painting the principles of three "far-offs" were shared. The three far-offs dealt with the problems of representing the far-off perpendicularly in elevation, far-off in depth, and far-off horizontally on a plane ground. To execute their magnificent waters and mountains paintings, the artists, constrained by the size of their drawing paper, used these three principles to render their splendid pictures of precipitous mountains and vast rivers or lakes. Garden designers faced an analogous problem in building rockeries in the limited space available in most private gardens. Chinese garden artists turned to the three far-offs of Chinese painting to solve their problem also. Thus, rockeries were usually designed with the higher peaks in the background and the lower in the foreground to give a sense of the mountains far-off in elevation; by interlocking two mountains to create the illusion of depth far-off; and to obtain the feeling of horizontal far-off by means of tortuous winding elevations, paths, etc.

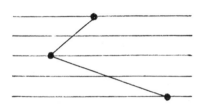

A

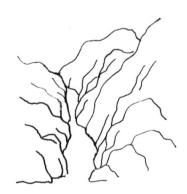

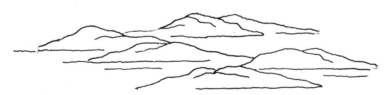

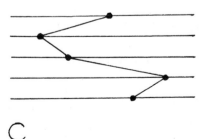

C

The "three long-range perspectives" in Chinese waters-and-mountains painting:
A. long-range perspective in height,
B. in depth and
C. in horizontal.

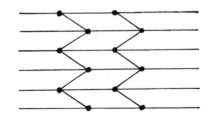

B

THE TEN TRADITIONAL METHODS OF PILING UP ROCKERIES AND HILLS

A. Tiao (single), pushing out
B. Tiao (double)
C. Piao (floating in the air)
D. Kua (spanning), the top stone stretched out
E. Xuan (hanging high in the air)
F. Chui (drooping in the air)
G. Dou (the slab-stones connected high in the air)
H. Ka (using smaller stones to support the huge mountain rocks).

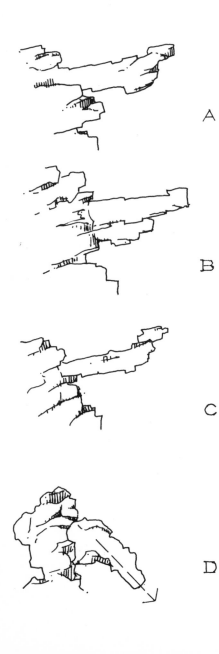

A

B

C

D

The ten technical methods used in the piling up of rockeries in traditional Chinese classical gardens were summarized in ten technical words: Tiao (pushing out), Piao (floating in the air), Tou (seeing through), Kau (spanning), Lian (linking), Xuan (hanging), Chui (drooping), Dou (arching), Ka (blocking), Jian (sword upwards).

Tiao, the method of pushing out, is executed by laying a rectangular slab of stone so that it extends outward from the face of the rockery into space and overhanging the lower slopes. This method is somewhat akin to the second method of floating in the air. The protruding part of the stone is called Tiao Tou, the pushing-out head. The stone is placed in such a way that the thinnest section protrudes while the thicker section is firmly located in the main body of the hill in order to keep the stone's center of gravity within the main body of the hill and assure the stability of both the rockery and the stone. Further, the stone is placed so that it has a slight upward thrust both to lend a tortuous feeling and further enhance stability. The stone selected for the slab should have a horizontal grain structure and possess a good-looking figure.

Piao is the method of placing a stone on the protruding end of a rectangular slabs of stone placed in the hill to create the image of floating in the air. The superimposed stone must have a grain structure and colour in accord with that of the slab. The careful matching of grain and colour will enhance the sense of a cloud floating in the air or an object floating on flowing water. The objective is to give a sense of lightness to the rockery and to create a harmony with the infinite space into which the slab and stone project.

Tou refers to the need to create the illusion of mountain passes that the viewer may see through to other mountains or beyond to the far-off landscape. Tou is less a construction method than a design objective. The objective is to help create a perception of extended space and to emphasize either the harmony of the rockery or to provide a contrast between the rockery and the scenes beyond.

Kua means specifically the stone used as the final element in the rockery. The selection and placement of this capping stone is very important to the esthetic integrity of the rockery. The stone used must harmonize with the stones used to finish the upper half of the rockery. It should stretch upward and outward at an angle like an outstretched arm pointing to the heavens. The objective is not only esthetic in properly completing the rockery but spiritual as a sign of the joining of heaven and earth.

Lian. The Lian method of piling-up rockeries makes for the truly remarkable and striking form of a false mountain. Long, flat stones of variant shapes and thickness are placed in ring-like structures, one on top of the other. The underlying structure is not unlike thin cakes piled one on the top of the other. But rather than a perfectly round structure, with perfectly straight sides, Lian are designed so that each layer protrudes or recedes from the vertical line established by the lower layers. This jagged outline replicates wild natural scenes. With the addition of well-executed waterfalls and the thoughtful planting of bent and weather-scarred trees and shrubs, awesome and compelling rockeries can be constructed.

Xuan refers to a method of piling-up rockeries which is related to and complements the Lian method. In the Xuan approach, however, flat stones of varying shapes and thickness are placed vertically. The placing of the stones and cementing them must be done carefully to insure the structural soundness of this form of false mountain. Like Lian the final form is very striking and well-suited to the construction of water effects of the most marvelous kind.

The **Chui** approach to constructing a rockery is somewhat similar to the Lian method in that flat stones are formed in a ring-like structure. It differs from Lian, however, in that the stones are placed so that they slope downward or droop as seen when drops of water freeze on sloping surfaces.

Dou refers to stone archways made to cross crevices in a rockery. Such archways not only add an exotic and unique feeling to a rockery but also function as bridges on the pathway leading up and around the hill. An archway is particularly effective when the crevasse which it spans also carries a watercourse.

Ka means the appropriate use of smaller stones to support and stabilize a huge stone. These smaller stones must be placed so as to leave crevices between them. A perceptual sense of simplicity and lightness must be the esthetic objective in placing Ka stones.

Jian refers to the need to place the mountain summit rock with the pointed end at the top and the bigger and heavier end at the base. This is interpreted as a sword pointing upward in the air but served the obvious practical purpose of maintaining the stability of the uppermost elements of the rockery.

E

F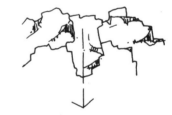

MOUNTAIN ROCKS PILED ACCORDING TO CERTAIN RULES

The famous early 12th century stonemason Chang Shan Shi compiled a set of guidelines which simply organized and codified the best of traditional practice. These guidelines dealt with the entire range of the use of rocks and stones in the art of gardening from the most simple to the most complex — from the proper placement of a single stone in a garden scene to the construction of elaborate "false mountains".

G

In his book *Oral Accounts Recorded* he emphasized the importance of an esthetically sensitive approach to the work of construction. Thus, the people involved in the actual building of a garden must be sensitive to the grain, colour, size, figure and angles of the rock employed in addition to the purely structural considerations involved in building a stable construction. The workmanship required keen sensitivity to esthetic considerations. No sign of man's handiwork

H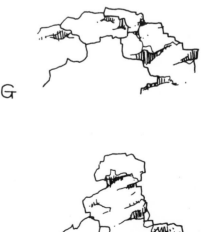

should be evident in a man-made garden mountain or rockery when it is completed. The rocks and stones used to create a rockery of even the most fantastic figure must seem to be a natural assemblage. To achieve this natural verisimilitude obviously demanded not only creative design but also exquisite craftsmanship in execution.

The simplest and most elementary use of stone in a garden is obviously that of rocks and stones used on the plane surface of the ground. Chinese landscape artists distinguished their layouts of this type — namely a single stone, a concentrated assemblage of stones and a scattered assemblage of stones.

If a single rock was to be used in a particular scene it must be especially fine in figure and size. The colour and grain must be harmonious with the native mountains. Its siting must be consistent with the proper regard for harmony and contrast in the scene. If on the other hand an outstanding and wonderful stone was available in the mass of stones brought from the local quarry, it could be the central element in a scene constructed to display its splendour. Single stone scenes are called Dan Dian (solitary spot scene) or Dan Jin (decorative rock scene). Such scenes are often used to set off a doorway or to provide a diverting decoration in front of a courtyard or under a window, at the side of a passageway or in a pond as an islet. The solitary rock is generally positioned in a direct line of sight. When a particularly lovely stone is discovered it is placed alone in a courtyard devoid of other rocks to heighten the viewer's appreciation. In this case, it is called Gushang Dan (a solitary rock in love). An example of Gushang Dan is located in the Yu Yuan Garden of Shanghai and is called Yu Linglong.

The concentrated style of rock scene is constructed of several rocks, usually from 2 to 10 pieces. The rocks are piled together quite closely with only enough earth to contain a few plants. This style of stone construction is called Ju Dian (concentrated spot). Rocks and stones of different sizes and shapes are arranged in an irregular and uneven pattern. Symmetrical layouts or even rows of rocks are strictly eschewed. The irregular sizes, shapes and asymmetric construction both vertically and horizontally lead to a sense of the natural configuration of a stone outcrop. Quite commonly the spaces left by the irregular concentrated style are filled with earth and a few shrubs or flowers planted in them to contrast with and relieve the cold and hard appearance of the stone. But their plantings must be used sparingly so the rock scene can be seen. A carefully laid out and constructed Ju Dian placed before a white wall planted with shrubs and plants chosen for their fine colour makes a striking scene reminiscent of a finer landscape painting on white drawing paper.

The scattered-type rock scene is called San Dian (scattered specks) in traditional Chinese landscaping. It is a style which must be carefully and tastefully used for, as with all simple esthetic expressions, it can be banal if not handled creatively. The scattered-rock style involves the placing of stones, singly or in small groups, at esthetically appropriate spots throughout a garden scene in a natural manner. These solid ornamental features are commonly placed at

Placladus orientalis

Guesthouse Garden scene

Cycas revoluta

Plate 3

Visitors in Bamboo Garden

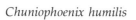

Chuniophoenix humilis

Bambusa ventricosa

Plate 4

pond side, under trees, along and in creeks, on embankments, at the foot of a hill and on slopes and roadsides. Some stones are erected perpendicularly, some laid horizontally, some lay half hidden in the earth as if a natural rock outcrop, some are positioned on an earthen hilltop like rocky peaks, some are scattered around or among architectural groups as solid ornaments. The great secret of the esthetically successful use of the scattered rock scene is to be found in the fact that the rocks are not laid at random but in harmony with the esthetic objectives of the scene and in accord with the topographic conditions of the site.

THE BUILDING OF "FALSE MOUNTAINS"

Chang distinguished between and described five major forms for the design and construction of rockeries. Each found its original model in natural formations and each were used as traditional forms in landscape painting and the art of gardening. The five forms are:

1. Jian Le Shi (Sword with Point Up). This form was used to recreate young upthrust mountains with strongly vertical features and precipitous slopes.
2. Baolei Shi (Fortress Type). This form was modelled after round multipeaked ranges of mountains. The domelike quality of old mountains sculpted to round smooth peaks by erosion and glaciation inspired this form.
3. Yunceng Shi (Cloud-layer Type). The natural prototype of this form is found in very old mountains, badly eroded to gentle slopes with the layers of deposited rock exposed only occasionally. The rocks buried halfway in the earth are like heads exposed above the ground. This type of rockery is constructed of piles of rectangular stone slabs with horizontal grains to enhance the perception of multiple layers of stone.
4. Pili Shi (Split Type). This form of rockery imitates the fantastic and unusual natural rock formations which are occasionally seen in badly eroded (whether by wind or water) areas. Some of the resulting formations are left at a slant. This striking formation appealed to the Chinese esthetic sensibility and so is commonly found in both gardens and paintings. Rectangular slabs of stone are placed so that one set of the parallel sides of the slabs slant in the same direction resulting in a rockery that slopes naturally on one side but on the opposite side creates a massive overhang.
5. Fule Shi (Axe with the Edge Downward). Another fantastic shape derived from natural formations seen in badlands. As the name implies the upper part of the rockery is thicker than the lower part. In this case opposite sides both create a rock overhang.

Mountain rocks laid out alongside the Xuan Wu Lake of Nanking.

The shapes of real mountains in nature.

Moulding of Rockery Peaks

As is evident, much of the character and esthetic intentions of a rockery are comprehended in the peak or ridge — Shan Feng in Chinese. Much care and attention, therefore, is devoted to both the design and the construction of the peak. The figure and angles of the rocks used on the top have to be consistent with the form of the rockery. Thus, the rocks used in the Jian Li Shi must possess an energetic perpendicular line. The uppermost rocks directly under the peak rocks are laid to reveal the varying and irregular layers from front to back. These lower rocks also have to be selected carefully to maintain the undulating (tortuous, convex and concave feature) figure at the sides.

The layout and disposition of the secondary peaks must be carefully controlled so that they not only are consistent with the form chosen for the primary peak but are also harmonious and act as a foil for beautifying and animating the rockery scene. Moreover, the secondary peaks must be designed not only with differences in size and elevation but also to provide differences in light and shade to enhance the image of the principle peak. All of these factors — movement, shape, size, elevation, light and shadow — must be integrated in relationship to the esthetic objective incarnate in the primary peak.

The Design and Disposition of Secondary Peaks

The multifamous demands made upon the garden artist in properly designing and integrating secondary peaks in rockeries lead to the naming and description of the various forms which they can take. The forms are:

1. Jian Pei (Laid Out as the Shape of a Sword). As the name implies this form of secondary peak must be laid out in accord with the highest peak of the Jian Li Shi form. The purpose of Jian Pei is to intensify the viewer's perception of the precipitous and heaven — pointing quality of the main peak.

2. Dun Pei (Laid Out as a Block of Stone). The purpose of this form of secondary peak is to provide a sense of a firm and stable base to the range. Thick square blocks of stone are laid beside the main peak in a simple and natural form to provide the feeling of a solid secondary peak. Dun Pei is frequently used with the Pili Shi and Fuli Shi forms of primary peak to provide a sense of stability to an intrinsically unstable form and a natural, indeed commonplace element, in a fantastic rockery.

3. Wo Pei (Laid Out as Lying). In this case large flat slabs of stone are placed in the direction opposite of the primary peak to give a feeling of greater balance and stability to the total rockery and also to create the impression of greater areal extent.

4. Dan Pei (Single Layout). In this form only a single secondary peak is used. This single secondary is usually only about 1/2 to 3/5 the height of the main peak. The Dan Pei is placed so that the contrasts of light and shade playing on the main peak are distinct and bold.

5 Shuang Pei (Double Layout). This form refers to a rockery laid out with two secondary peaks. The two secondaries must not be equal in

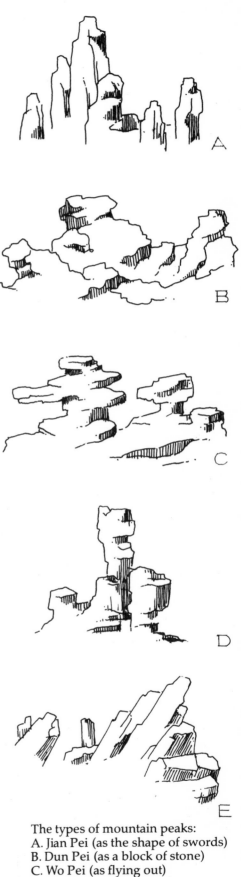

The types of mountain peaks:
A. Jian Pei (as the shape of swords)
B. Dun Pei (as a block of stone)
C. Wo Pei (as flying out)
D. Dan Pei (single layout)
E. Duo Pei (slant-layout).

size or height, although both must be lower than the main peak. The three peaks in the group should not be positioned along the same line of sight, so that each may contribute to and intensify the ornamental effects of the separate scenes based around each. Obviously all the esthetic objectives underlying the use of a three peak rockery must be observed and kept intact in so far as the range considered by itself is concerned.

6. Duo Pei (Multiple Layout). This form refers to all rockeries which are designed to use three or more secondary peaks. The main concern in laying out Duo Rei is to refrain from putting all the peaks in the same line of sight or arranged in rows. As in all rockeries, all secondary peaks must be laid out with unequal heights and at varying distances from one another.

As Ji Cheng said in his famous gardening book *Yuan Zhi:* "A multiple peak rockery should not be tidy or like a pen rack. Rather the peaks must undulate continuously and always in accord with the natural rhythm and flow of natural mountains. Multiple peak rockeries must be piled irregularly and unevenly."

Other Considerations in Piling-up Rockeries

Rockeries, no matter how carefully designed and constructed, will look monotonous and sterile if the many surface features which regularly are found in natural mountains are not also replicated. These natural features include cliffs, caves, ravines, and rock heads. False mountains must be designed to incorporate these features if the rockery is to be perceived as authentic and in harmony with the natural order of things.

Overhanging Cliffs

In *Yuan Zhi* Ji Cheng said: "To make an attractive, breathtaking scene, overhanging cliffs should be built into the rockery." The building of an overhanging cliff involves the same structural and masonry techniques used in building the Pili Shi or slanting hill form of primary peak, as the footing is smaller than the overhanging head. The foundation must be firm and heavy. Large slabs of stone must be used in piling up the rockery to maintain the solidity of the overhang. Lighter slabs are used near the top and laid with a greater overhang so as to maintain the stability of the overhanging cliff.

Cliffs

A vertical cliff is like a rock split with an axe. The cliff is never a single vertical surface up its entire length. Rather the higher faces are set in from the lower face. Thus, to replicate a cliff in a rockery, long slabs of stone are fixed perpendicularly along a narrow side, with each successive vertical slab stepped in from the lower.

Stone Caves

Stone caves serve a dual purpose in rockeries. They not only duplicate an intriguing feature of natural mountains but are also used as passageways through the rockery for the use of viewers. When used

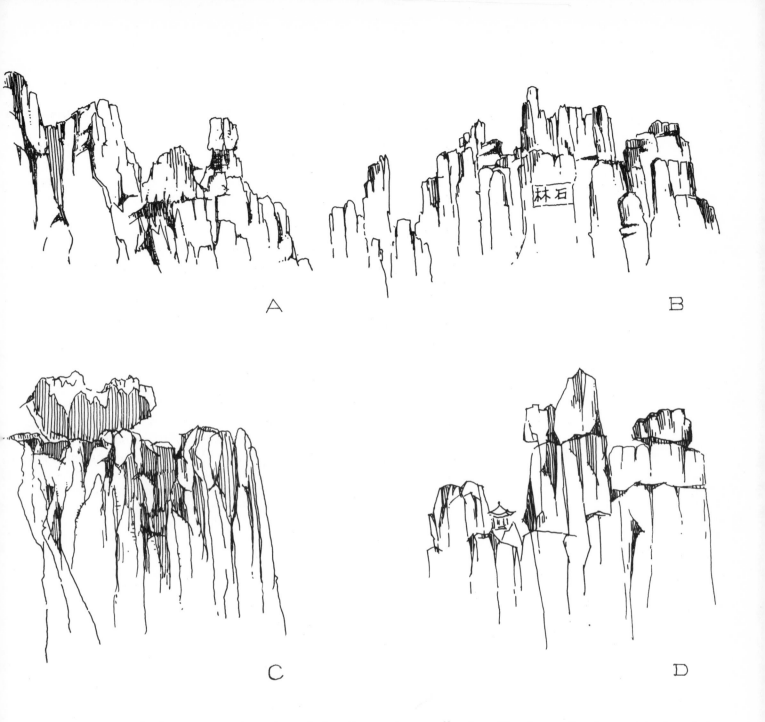

A

B

石林

C

D

as passageways, windows may be pierced in the outer wall at appropriate places to view a scene either on the rockery or in the garden below. Caves used as passageways help provide a sense of a large garden.

In building caves the rockery walls must be thick and firm enough to support the cave roof and the rockery above the cave. Either stone lintel or keyed arch construction techniques must be used to make the roof. A variant of the stone is called San Dong (mountain cave).

Encircling

A variant of the stone cave is called Huan (encircling). Encircling means a false cave — an indentation in the face of the mountain without a tunnel or room. Encircling features are used mainly to provide variety to the face of the rockery but may also be used to pro-

The shapes of real mountains in nature:
A. Qi Tuo Shao Nu (young girl riding on camel)
B. Shi Lin (forest of stones)
C. Yun Jian Shi Lianhua (lotus in the cloud)
D. Cai Yun Shen Chu (colourful clouds in depth).

vide passing space on a rockery path or to provide a setting for a small exquisite scene of mountain plants.

Both real and encircling caves are designed to present the views from the "false mountain" in one of two ways. The first is to create a positive break in a scene and is called Zheng Duan. The object is to construct the cave so that a scene suddenly pops into or disappears from full, clear view as the viewer enters or leaves a particular point in the cave.

The other, Cuo Duan, is designed to prepare the viewer for an approaching or receding scene by breaking the approaches to the scene with intermittent, vertical jagged stones or plantings. In this way the scene is only intimated by occasional preliminary or terminal glimpses through the vertical elements. In only a single spot may the visitor clearly view the scene in an unimpeded view.

Ravine

Ravines in rockeries, as in natural mountains, are of two kinds — a cleft running down the side of a mountain and a low, narrow passage or pass between two peaks. In the first case, the ravine is created to give the side of the rockery variety and/or to provide a site for an unusual and exquisite plant scene. In the latter case the entrance to the ravine is exposed on the mountainside but the scenes beyond can only be seen when the viewer has passed through it. Ravines are one of the most important features of rockeries and should be designed as such.

FOUR AVOIDANCES IN PILING ROCKERIES

The proper (in the sense of adhering to natural models) and esthetically satisfying design and construction of rockeries will be enhanced by avoiding the four most common mistakes made in the past.

First of all, the rocks and stones used for piling rockeries should be of the same colour and grain pattern. Thus, for example, lake stones are widely admired for their exquisite colours, grain patterns and variety in figure and shape. But lake stones vary greatly in these qualities so it is necessary to carefully select the stones for the specific qualities required for piling up a particular rockery. The rockeries in the paintings of the famous artists Guo Xi of the Song Dynasty (11th century) and Wang Meng of the Yuan Dynasty (14th century) favored round lake stones piled up in rockeries.

Sedimentary stones are noted for their forcefulness and dignity. They usually have a marked and uniform grain structure. Regular smooth slabs can easily be obtained from this form of stone. The plane surface of the slab is harmonious with the horizontal grain pattern. When strongly grained sedimentary rocks are used for both horizontal and perpendicular surfaces a beautiful pattern of rock, fine edges and sharp corners are clearly visible and achieve a splendid result. The rockeries in the paintings drawn by Ma Yuan of the Song Dynasty (12th century) and Ni Zan of the Yuan Dynasty (14th century) were piled up of sedimentary stones that were cut nearly in a square-shape. These two kinds of stones (lake and sedimentary) are quite different and should not be mixed in use.

Rockeries piled up with either selected pond/lake stones or sedimentary stone slabs are equally beautiful and satisfying. As we have seen, two artists in each of two dynasties preferred one to the other. The important point, however, is that once selected, the choice of stone should be strictly adhered to.

Secondly, stones of the same kind may not have the same grain pattern. Therefore, it is necessary to choose only those of nearly the same pattern for a specific rockery.

Thirdly, avoid evenness in placing stones in the rockery. The stones used in piling up rockeries should be different in size and height and placed randomly to avoid any hint of evenness or stones in rows whether horizontally or vertically.

Finally, avoid using too many small stones (less than 20 cm in diameter). In piling up rockeries, use big stones (35 cm or larger) to promote a feeling of stability, firmness and large size. Small stones should be used only as filling stones between the big stones.

The entrance of Yi Yuan Garden.

Scenes of Pipa
(Loquat) Garden of
Zhou Zheng Yuan
Garden, Soochow.

Small courtyard scenes of Liu Yuan Garden, Soochow.

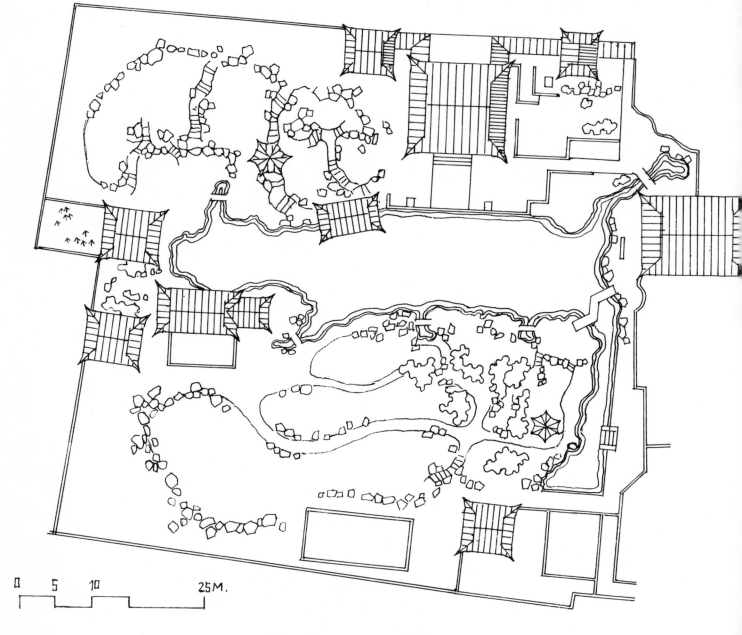

General plane figure of Qiu Xia Pu (Rosy Autumn
Clouds Garden) in Jia Ding County near Shanghai.

0   5   10   25M.

6 The Art of Water Gardening

Chinese gardening art relates closely to the water and mountains found in Nature, but does not simply imitate the types of scenery to be found in natural settings. Rather the art of the gardener is an expression of the artistic ideas and conceptions which emerge from the intimate and profound understanding of and feeling for Nature and natural processes.

LANDSCAPING WITH WATER

The classic Chinese gardening book *Yuan Zhi* speaks of "Shui Fa" (method of water gardening) and "Shan Fa" (method of mountain gardening). The writer, Ji Cheng, observed that "Water is laid out in accord with the shapes of the mountain range so watercourses follow the mountains." In keeping with this observation, the first consideration in selecting a suitable site for establishing a garden is to locate a good water source. An ancient Chinese saying points out that "waters are like the eyes in Nature while mountains are the eyebrows." Water in short, is a vital element in building a Chinese garden.

In Nature, water is found in a variety of forms, shapes and actions: rivers, lakes, creeks, ponds, waterfalls, springs, marshes, etc. In planning and designing, the first step is to study and understand the "to-and-fro" or activity of native water sources.

The waterscapes of the Summer Palace in Beijing were based on several natural water sources, but beautified by the earthwork of man-made piled up hills formed with the surplus soil excavated to enlarge the natural water surfaces into a single large lake. To build a waterscape in this way is to obtain twice the result with half the effort in classical Chinese gardening.

The well-known Soochow classical garden, the Zhou Zheng Yuan Garden, is also a splendid waterscape garden. Its original site was a

General plane figure of the Summer
Palace in Beijing:
A. Kunming Lake
B. South Lake
C. West Lake
D. Rear Lake
E. Dragon's King Temple Islet
F. West Embankment.

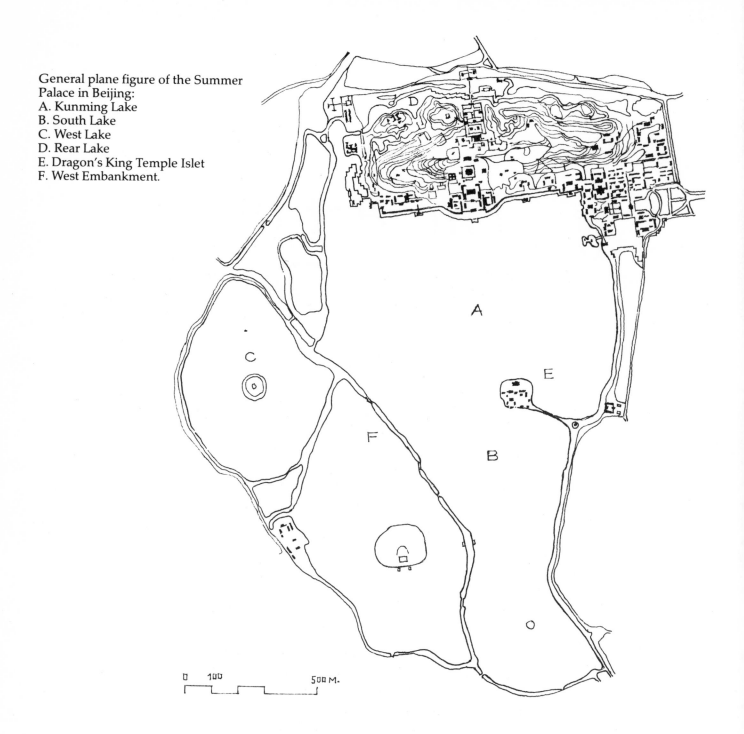

0 100   500 M.

marshy lowland which was deepened into several ponds. The surplus
earth was used to balance the pond by utilizing it to pile up a small
hill and rockery. Hills and waters are the essential elements underlying good garden design. Only when these elements are in place
should trees, bushes and flowers and the ornamental garden architecture such as pavilions, corridors, bridges, enclosing walls and
meandering paths be incorporated to compose a picturesque and
pleasing garden.

The two principles of guiding the artistic treatment of waters are
"Ju" (gathering together of water) and "Fen" (separation of waters).
At their simplest Ju refers to developing a plentiful supply of water

for landscaping large gardens while Fen defines the art used in landscaping small residence gardens. In the latter case, the esthetic objective is to separate water into small ponds, adding decorative rockeries, garden pavilions, halls and little bridges to form a secluded environment within enclosing walls.

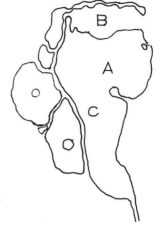

The Layout of Water Scenes

The use of extensive and large bodies of water in ancient Chinese gardens can be traced back to the reign of the Emperor Zhou Wen Wang in the 11th century B.C. Zhou's favorite recreation was to raise fish in the palace fishpond called Ling Zhao (Efficacious Marsh). Thereafter, the Kunming Pond was excavated by Emperor Han Wu Di of Han Dynasty to create a lake of sufficient size for recreational yachting. From the 14th century onward, a number of well-known watercourses were excavated for various emperors of the Ming and Qing Dynasties in the imperial palace gardens. They include the Three Seas (North-Middle-South Seas), the Fu Hai (Fortune Sea) of the Yuan Ming Yuan, and the Kunming Lake of the Summer Palace in Beijing; the West Lake of Hangchow and the Nan Hu (South Lake) of Jia Xing near Shanghai. These bodies of water are variously styled: "Hai, Hu, Zhao, or Chi" (Sea, Lake, Marsh, Pond). They are the main motif or focus in the garden as they provide a relatively "still space" as well as esthetic re-creation of natural scenes.

Islands of various sizes are almost always built in these large bodies of water to balance and relieve the monotony of the broad flat surfaces, as well as to reproduce the islands which occur in nature. Some of the more beautiful and better known islands in Beijing are the Qiong Hua (Gorgeous Jade) Islet in Bei Hai (North Sea) Park, the Long Wang Miao (Dragon Kings Temple) Islet in Kunming Lake in the Summer Palace and the Penglai Yaotai (Jade Abode of Immortals) Islet in the Fu Hai (Fortune Sea) of Yuan Ming Yuan. The smallest of these is only a decorative pavilion built over the water on a rock and earth footing.

Some islands are solitary while others are connected to other islands on the land by long bridges or green embankments. Watercourses are sited to take advantage of cloudy far-off hills or fields. The faint reflections of these borrowed scenes or the vast sky shining on the surface, together with the images of the decorative garden architecture located at the water's edge, yield a view of great beauty in well designed waterscapes. Some waterscapes are designed to bring the sky and water together in one placid scene.

Along the surrounding edges and banks, decorative scenic spots of hollow rocks, trees, shrubs and flowers are artfully located. Alternatively, the embankment may be enhanced with irregular courses of cobbles while shoals of reefs are dotted in the water near the water edge. Here waterfowl find their favorite habitat. Such natural scenes are full of poetic flavor and picturesque atmosphere.

In Chinese waterscape gardening, the waters are sometimes separated into several areas at different elevations so the water falls as

Kunming Lake of the Summer Palace in Beijing and the West Lake in Hangchow:
A. Kunming Lake
B. Longevity Hill
C. West Embankment
D. West Lake
E. Little Isolated Hill
F. Su's Embankment
G. San Tan Yin Yue (Moon-in-three Ponds).

a thin, shimmering screen crossed by a bridge. Such a wonderful water-screen scene makes a fantastic view when seen from afar. A fine example of this water design is to be seen at the Chengteh Mountain Resort. The water passage joining the Upper Lake to the Lower Lake is formed as a long and broad water screen. Above this iridescent fall a long pavilion-bridge has been built. The artistic treatment of water in this way is called "Hua Jing Wei Dong" (to make still water move).

Water can be used to a variety of satisfying esthetic ends in gardening. A vast water surface is bright and reflects spectacular borrowed scenes; the sounds of a murmuring stream are known and enjoyed by all; clouds reflected in water create varied shapes continually changing, and waterfalls sparkle in the light from both the sun and the moon. Water can be well used as a mirror. Beautiful images vividly reflect in the water — sunset and sunrise, the surrounding landscapes, and the picturesque scenes comprised of decorative architecture, ornamental trees and flowers.

In small gardens, the perception of water can be extended and deepened by making small irregular watercourses. Small decorative islets, pavilions and connecting bridges will divert the viewer's line of vision. The same perceptual illusion of extensive space can be achieved at less cost by making curving and bending paths and sight lines coordinated with the irregular shorelines.

THE FOUR KINDS OF PONDS

Four kinds of ponds are distinguished in Chinese gardening design. They differ in shape, size, gathering together of water (Ju) or separation of water (Fen), in keeping with the esthetic intention of the pond.

Ribbon shape. The ribbon-shape pond is, as its name implies, narrow and bends like a ribbon. It is commonly used as a foil for rockeries. The author of *Yuan Zhi* points out that the site should be selected with a view to the water supply; for example: "Before digging the foundation one should investigate the sources and note the flow of the water, conduct the stream like a curve or ribbon through the grounds. Such a waterway cannot be completely surveyed or measured in a glance from any one point."

Squarely-circular shape. The squarely-circular shaped pond is based on a relatively large square watersurface. Decorative architecture of water-kiosks and bridges conceal the four corners to give a circular appearance to the pond. The captivating and fascinating atmosphere of the waterscape is best seen from the kiosks and bridges. Wang Shi Yuan Garden of Soochow has a good example of this form of waterscape.

Narrow-shaped pond. The narrow-shaped pond is long, narrow

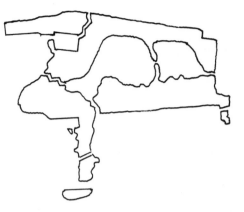

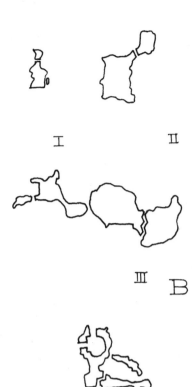

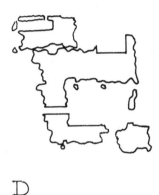

I

I   II

II

III   B

A   III

C   D

I

II

The different shapes of ponds in the classical gardens of Soochow.
A. Squarely-round form:
(1) Wang Shi Yuan Garden's ponds, (2) Yi Pu (Nursery of Arts), (3) Liu Yuan Garden's ponds.
B. Narrow-rectangular forms: (1) Hu Yuan Garden's pond, (2) Pond in Liu's semicircular-form residence-garden, (3) Yi Yuan Garden's pond.
C. Belt-like forms: (1) Huan Xiu Shanzhunag (All Beautiful Surrounding Mountain Villa).
D. Ponds-in-group: (1) Zhou Zheng Yuan Garden's ponds, (2) Lion Grove Garden's ponds.

and nearly straight. At the ends or the narrowest part small crossing bridges are placed to enhance the esthetic effect. In the Ji Chang Yuan Garden of Wusih, a pond of this shape is the principal waterscape feature of the garden.

Grouped ponds. In the Soochow classical gardens, which are typically small residential gardens, grouped ponds are widely used. It is in these gardens that the Fen principle is most widely employed and historically from which the principle was derived. To create a perceptual illusion of greater expanse, the ponds are excavated in different shapes and sizes. Thus, in the Yi Yuan Garden, the grouped ponds are formed by separating a long narrow water surface into several parts connected by bridges and banks. A different means of grouping ponds is displayed in the Lion Grove Garden, where separate ring-shaped ponds were dug. The Zhou Zheng Yuan Garden employs yet another means of grouping ponds. The main garden is actually a single waterscape garden. However, at the central point of the pond the bridges and dikes which cross the pond join in a large land mass. Upon this central land area decorative buildings and superb plantings of trees and flowers have been placed to shape out a beautiful waterscape of several grouped ponds.

Sectional and cross section drawing of Xiao Cang Lang of Zhou
Zheng Yuan Garden viewing southwards.

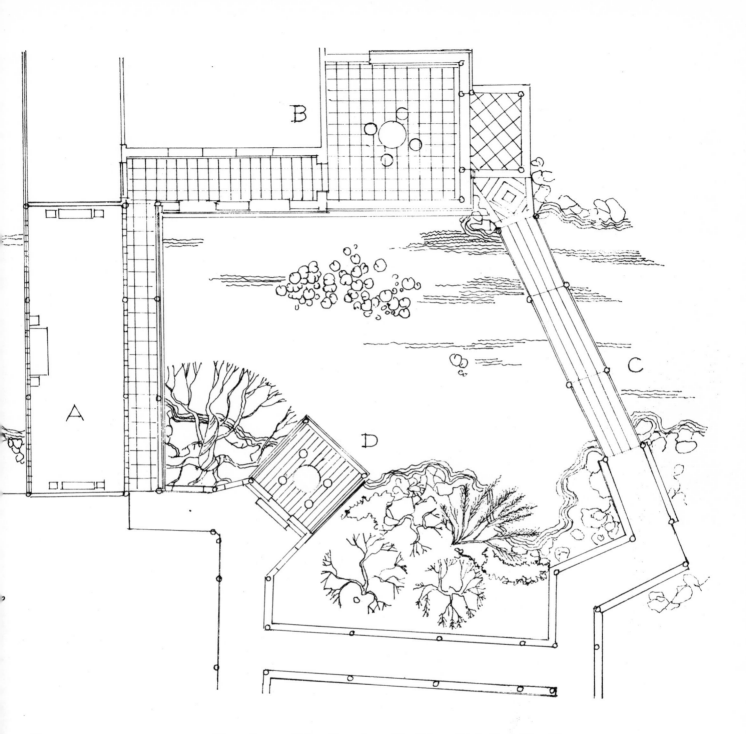

Plane figure of Xiao Cang Lang Shui Yuan (Little Dark Blue Wave
Water-courtyard) of Zhou Zheng Yuan Garden in Soochow:
A. Xiao Cang Lang
B. De Zhen Ting (Gained-truth Pavilion)
C. Xiao Fei Hong (Little Flying Rainbow Pavilion)
D. Ting Song Feng (Listening Sough in the Pines).

The Art of Water Gardening   91

Upper left, a pond scene in the western part of Zhou Zheng Yuan Garden, Soochow; *Upper right*, a water-gate of Yi Yuan Garden, Soochow; *Lower*, a pond in the middle part of Zhou Zheng Yuan Garden.

Upper left, a small water-course scene of Liu Yuan Garden, Soochow; *Upper right,* a water scene with a small wooden bridge in Zhou Zheng Yuan Garden, Soochow; *Lower,* early summer on West Lake, Hangchow.

The Art of Water Gardening 93

Sectional and longitudinal section drawing of Xiao Cang Lang (Small Blue-wave) Water-courtyard, viewing westward.

WATERSCAPE TREATMENT

Waterscapes are divided into two kinds in the traditional art of Chinese landscaping: the moving water of waterfalls, fountains and springs located on cliffs and creeks; the still water of ponds, pools and lakes. By ingenious gardening with water, exquisite waterscapes can be designed as required by local conditions and the nature and extent of the water source.

The extraordinary versatility which artificial waterfalls offer the designer to create a variety of water scenes and effects which replicate the patterns of nature, is unmatched by any other single element in the garden. The form and effects of water screens are determined by the positioning of the rocks at the head and foot of the falls. Falls may fall in a single straight screen or in several separated channels. These falls may terminate in a dynamic splashing or fall gently into a quiet pool. Whatever the design and effect of the fall and its receiving pool the total effect on the viewer is enhanced not only by the sight but also the natural and soothing sounds of moving water.

The size and flow of waterfalls must be consistent with the volume of water available from the water source. If a large volume is available a thick plunging waterfall can be created. If, on the other hand, the rate of flow is relatively small, the waterfall should be made on a gentle incline and the flow of water be broken as it flows over an irregular surface, such as that in the Xie Qu Yuan Garden's waterfall in the Summer Palace of Beijing. Here, the water flows bubbling down into the lotus pond. A flat bridge crosses the gently flowing falls. This fascinating scene reminds the beholder of a real valley found in nature. If the waterfall flows in several separate sections, the sections should not be of equal length but rather of unequal ranges. Such a falls may be seen in front of the Fei Quan Ting (Flying-fountain Pavilion) in the Lion Grove Garden of Soochow.

All waterfalls whether narrow or broad, single or multiple, steep or gentle must be clothed with appropriate plantings. Pine, cypress, maple trees and vines should be planted alongside. To add to the beauty and imitate nature shoals and pools should be incorporated in the total layout.

Falling Water

Luo Shui (Falling Water) refers to the design and making of water-falls. Size, length, section and layer produce specific artistic visual and sound effects in the garden. In Chinese gardening practice water-falls are classified by shape and type as follows:

Falling straight down. When the water falls in a narrow turbulent band at a long distance from the lip of the falls and hits rocky ground, splashing drops in all directions, it is called Zhu Luo (Column-shaped Falls). When the band of water is thin and screen-like the fall is called Pian Luo (Sheet-shaped Falls). If the falling water hits rocks midway in its drop and the water splashes in all directions, the fall is called San Luo (Splashing-shaped Falls).

Linear falls. When a garden lacks a good steady water source resort is had in creating a waterfall to Xian Luo (Linear Falls). The water source for this type of falls comes from a false mountain on rainy days. The rain water is collected on the mountain by careful design of the mountain peak and then is channeled to drop in linear form in front of grottos like strings of pearls.

Falling from the left and right sides. In this type of waterfalls water comes from the steep hills flowing through an inclined channel in a zigzag fashion from the left and to the right sides of the channel through trees, shrubs and grass to form a wilderness water scene.

Falls in layers. Die Luo (Falls in Layers) designates a stepped falls. The water falls perpendicularly to a basin or pond from which it flows to the next falls. Two or more sections or steps may be constructed. The height of the separate falls should be different to avoid a monotonous feeling and to create a perception of a natural water course. Die Luo is most typically used on terraces or gently sloping false mountain sides.

Pools

The final element of all waterfalls is the pool into which the water drops. It is called Shui Tan (Pool). In designing the pool the water may either fall on rocks to create a splashing effect or directly onto the surface of the pool. The pool must be large enough that a part of the surface is always smooth so the viewer may see the bottom decorated with rocks and gravel and the small fish which should be introduced. The banks should be planted with lush grasses and low growing water-loving plants. Water plants may be planted in the pool if it is of sufficient size.

Creeks and Gullies

Xi (Creek) as the name implies is a relatively slow moving water course carrying water down the side of a mountain. Jian (Gulley) refers to sections of a creek marked by a swift, turbulent flow. In Hangchow there is a well-known scenic spot called Jiu Xi Shi Ba Jian (Nine Creeks and Eighteen Gullies) that is a natural waterscape. Such natural scenic spots formed the model and inspiration for the creeks and gullies which are widely and well used in Chinese gardens.

Superb creeks can be created in false mountains if they are designed to flow through rocky and wooded parts of the mountain to end at the sandy beach of a pond. The pleasant gurgling of the stream as it passes over its gravel bed only enhances the viewer's pleasure. Pavilions and galleries are established on the banks of the creek to view the creek and its bordering gardens and to enjoy the music of the water. A particularly artful pattern of water gardening with creeks and gullies is to be found in the Huan Xiu Shan Zhuang (Beautiful Surrounding Mountain Villa) of Soochow.

Plane sketch map of Ba Yin Jian of Ji Chang Yuan Garden in Wusih.

Creeks and gullies should be designed with continually changing elevations so that the flow changes from one section to the next, intermittently rushing down a steep gully and then slowing as the creek changes to a nearly level bed. Further, creeks and gullies should follow meandering, bending, zigzag courses. Sometimes they should branch, only to be rejoined with no branching or confluence appearing the same. Such a splendid water gardening pattern can be seen in the Ji Chang Yuan Garden of Wusih. Here the Ba Yin Jian (Eight-Musical-South Gully) of the garden is laid out at the foot of Wei Shan Mountain. A fountain forms a stream flowing down through a bending gully of hollow rocks, thence into a clear pool and finally flies over a waterfall with a variety of small, clever waterscenes interspersed in the flow. The gully gets its name because the water as it strikes differently shaped hollow rocks produces sounds reminiscent of musical instruments playing eight tones. Finally the water falls into Jin Wei Pool. This gardening method is called Hua Wu Sheng Wei You Sheng (to make the soundless water become musical tunes).

Various ways of laying rocks in the creeks are described in the classical Chinese gardening literature. The proper use of rocks in the construction of a creek bed greatly enhances not only the structural durability of the bed but also the natural beauty of the creek. Chinese gardening defines five uses and positions for laying rock in the stream bed.

1. Rocks laid in the bottom with the broad face pointed upstream are called Ying Liu Dan (rock to ward off stream). They are used to resist and slow down the flow of turbulent water.
2. The stones laid on both sides of the stream are called Hu An Dan (bank-protect stones).
3. The stones laid at the bends of a creek to prevent erosion or washing away of the inside and outside banks are called Bao Jian Dan (corner stones).
4. Some rocks should be firmly embedded in the bottom and placed half-exposed in the stream to divide the flowing water into two channels. Such rocks are called Fen Liu Dan (rock to divide flowing water).
5. The pebbles laid at the bottom of the stream are called Pu Di Dan (bedding stones). The entire bottom of the bed should be lined with stones. The best looking stones are laid above the inferior ones. Sometimes cobbles are used instead of pebbles.

Fountains and Sheer-cliff Wells

The installation of fountains and sheer-cliff wells (springs) in the garden adds much beauty to a garden view as they vitalize the atmosphere in the landscapes. Very long ago, about the 1st century during the reign of Han Wu Di of the Han Dynasty, there was an embryonic form of a fountain called Tong Long Tu Shui (Copper Dragon Spitting Water) in his Gan Quan Yuan Garden (Sweet Fountain Garden). In the fresco of Yuan Dynasty, fountains were also found in the pictures.

But the classic fountain in the man-made mountain scenes is the Yu Quan Shan (The Mountain of the Jade Fountain), situated some kilometers from the Summer Palace. It is, according to Chinese tradition, the finest of "the eight views" or scenes of natural beauty in the environs of Beijing. The spot derives its name from the fact that the water gushing from the mountain is as pure and clear as jade.

No one who has visited the place will deny that the tradition is well founded. It is scarcely possible to point out any spot in the vicinity of Beijing more favored by Nature. The vegetation is luxuriant, almost superabundant. In a setting of magnificent old trees and in the midst of the verdure, the fresh fountain water feeds into the crystal-clear Kunming Lake of the Summer Palace.

According to tradition, the emperor Chang Zong of the Jin Dynasty (1190-1208) had a hunting pavilion erected there. This has long since disappeared, but there are two memorial tablets, one of them provided with the following inscription by the Emperor Qian Long (1736-1795): "The finest spring under heaven".

From documents that have come down it appears that the Emperor Qian Long employed hundreds of gardeners to improve the scenes of Jade Fountain still further, but the guiding principle on both occasions was evidently to adapt the design as far as possible to local conditions, and to follow the indications given by Nature.

The art of laying out a traditional Chinese garden lies in bringing together in an unaffected way the fundamental feature of the natural landscape that contains many kinds of hills and mountains, the verdure, the shade, the views; and the waterscape that contains the waterfalls, the winding streams, the natural pools, the fountains and the sheer-cliff wells from which water bubbles out, making an attractive scene in Nature.

THE ARRANGEMENT OF ISLETS

Both in imperial palace gardens and private residence gardens, islets in lakes or ponds are one of the main elements of Chinese gardening. These islets are often fairy islands. Talented artists and gardeners with their intimate feeling for nature, laid out islets modelled after nature in man-made lakes and ponds. They built pavilions, bridges and banks on different levels to enable the viewer to see both the distant borrowed scene outside the garden and the waterscapes in the garden.

The islets are also used to divide the water surface into distinct areas in order to relieve the monotonous appearance of long stretches of water. From the islets the waterside landscapes can be appreciated in every direction while from the waterside, the islets with their decorative architecture, ornamental trees and shrubs provide a picturesque focus for the waterscape. Islets and watersides mutually borrow scenes from each other in a splendid way.

The Different Shapes of Islets

The Chinese traditional landscape canon identifies five distinct types of islets:

1. Hilly islets (Shan Dao) are considered the finest form in as much as they provide an ideal contrast with the flat water surfaces. Hilly islets are of two types. The first is the gradually rising earth hill such as the Qiong Hua (Splendidly Jewelled) Islet of Bei Hai (North Sea) in Beijing and the Solitary Hill in the West Lake of Hangchow. The other type is the steep, rugged, rocky islets such as Jiao Shan and Xiao Gu Shan in the Yangtse River. Both types of islet present a strong vertical line which makes an esthetically satisfying contrast to the horizontal water line.

2. Plane ground islets (Ping Dao) are small pieces of land formed by sands naturally accumulated in rivers such as the Parrot Islet in the Yangtse River. In Chinese gardening, such small pieces of land in a lake or pond are piled up above the water level by dredging sand from the lake bed. Such artificial islets have sloped banks. They are typically planted with weeping willow trees and reeds which serve to make the islet as natural as those in the wilderness.

Lingyin (Soul's Retreat) Temple, tucked away in the mountains north of West Lake, Hangchow.

3. Projecting islets are called Ji Dao. They are really a peninsula jutting out into the water from the land. Frequently a huge rock placed at the end of the peninsula overhangs the water somewhat like a precipitous cliff.

4. A unique form of pond islet is called Chi Dao. It consists of a group of ponds and their defining embankments. The San Tan Yin Yue (Three Ponds Reflecting the Moon) in the West Lake of Hangchow represents this type of islet. Overall, it appears as a big island surrounded by water when seen from afar. However, it really consists of a series of separate ponds contained in a complicated embankment system. Old weeping willow trees planted along the embankments partly block the line of sight to help create the perception of a large island. However, once the viewer enters the garden and moves among the scenic spots, he feels as if these varied water scenes are "islets in a lake and lakes around islets". The individual scenes are sometimes closed and sometimes open in keeping with the remarkable ability of Chinese garden artists to achieve various spatial perceptions in the design and construction of traditional gardens.

5. The Gu Shang Dao (decorative solitary islet) is created by carefully placing a very large handsome rock in a pond or lake at the foot of a false mountain. The large rock is positioned to appear as if it is an outline of the hill. As the water surface rises and falls through the seasons, the Gu Shang Dao is sometimes partly and sometimes wholly exposed above the water level. This form of islet finds its inspiration in the everchanging and inspiring islets found in China's large rivers and seasonally fluctuating lakes. Solitary islets are usually positioned to relate harmoniously with waterside garden architecture.

The Positions of Islets

It is best to position islets to one side of the lake or pond rather than in the geometrical center. In the Fu Hai (Fortune Sea) of Yuan Ming Yuan, the Pen Dao Yao Tai (Jade Abode of Immortals) is placed in the center of the lake but three islets of different shape and size are cunningly grouped along an irregular line which directs the viewer's perception of the view away from the central position. In this way the monotony and triteness of the main islet is offset.

In natural settings the headwater of a lake is commonly marked by a natural accumulation of sand to form sandbars where the flow of the stream is slowed by big rocks. In the same fashion, it is advantageous to lay out a miniature delta in man-made lakes where the creek flows into the lake. These islets are then connected with bridges and embankment.

A water kiosk of the palace-garden in Nanking.

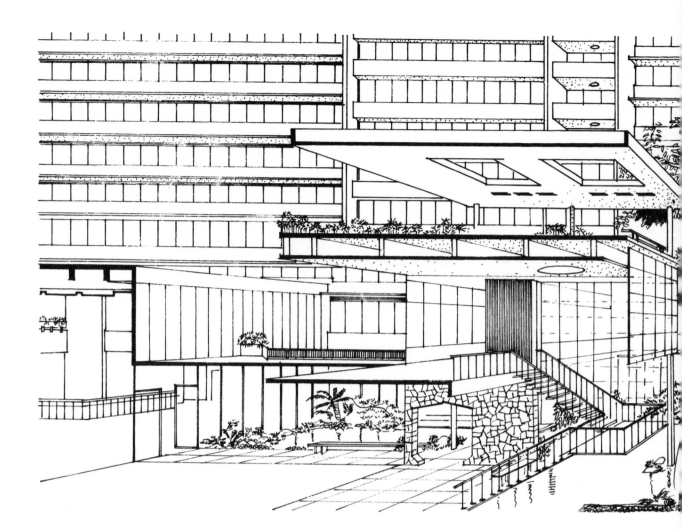

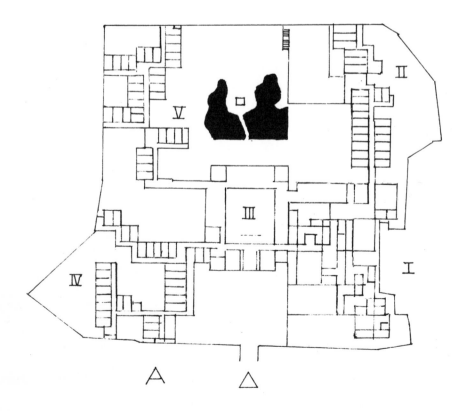

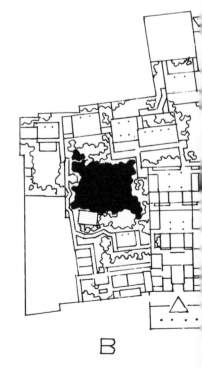

A △ B

100   *The Garden Art of China*

Perspective cross section of Bai Yun Bin Guan (White Cloud Guest House) in Canton.

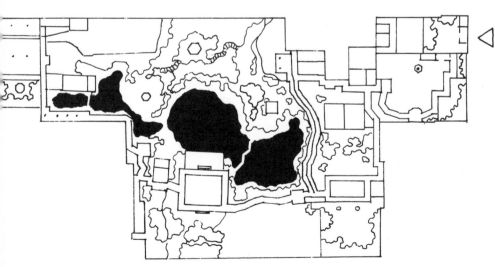

C

Some hotels in Beijing in contrast to the two Chinese classical gardens: Wang Shi Yuan Garden and Yi Yuan Garden of Soochow. A. Five areas of hotels in Beijing. B. Wang Shi Yuan Garden of Soochow. C. Yi Yuan Garden of Soochow.

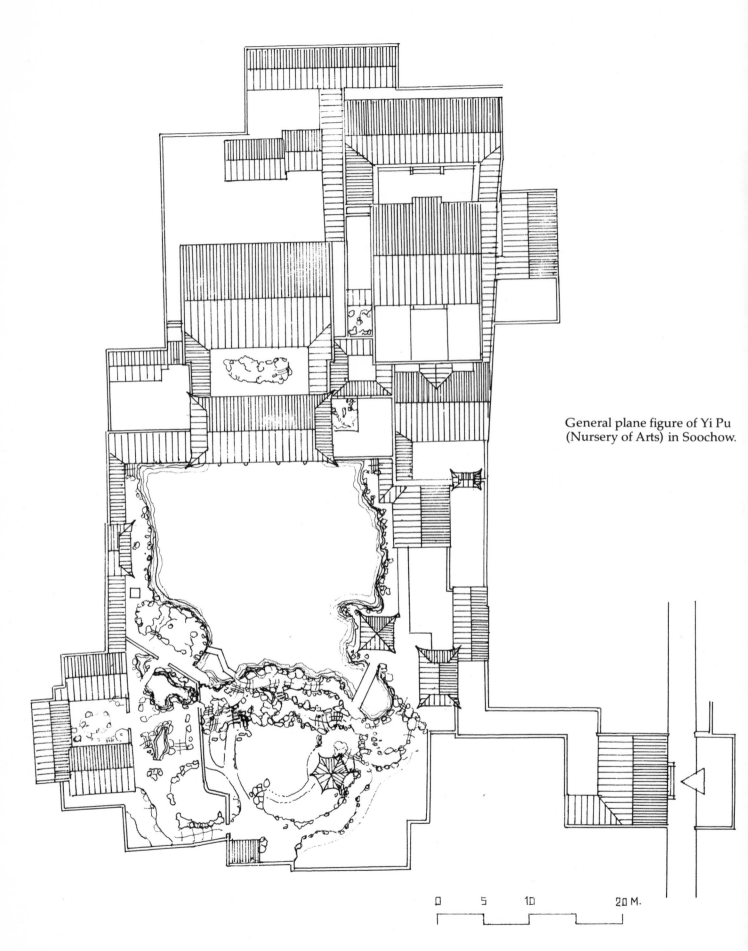

General plane figure of Yi Pu
(Nursery of Arts) in Soochow.

7 *Garden Architecture*

Buildings and other architectural structures are essential features in Chinese gardens. They fill not only the functional and practical roles universally associated with buildings, but also are of great ornamental value if sited and designed in harmony with cliffs, rockeries, water features, trees and flowers to achieve remarkable artistic effects reflecting the beauty of Nature. Amid winding paths the glassy stillness of ponds and the verdure of the plantings, the pavilions, kiosks, bridges and galleries providing for the interplay of light and shade must blend harmoniously with the other compositional elements.

The layout of structures requires openness, clearness, ease and gracefulness. The interplay between courtyards, open galleries, grottos, ornamental windows and doors, balustrades and perspective screens carefully integrated with scenic spots, creates an organic whole in the Chinese garden.

HALLS

The main hall is used in China as the place to receive guests, to conduct poetry writing parties, and in general for formal occasions. The space in front of the main hall is usually rectangular in shape. A pond situated in front of the hall with a piled-up rockery behind it is a classic traditional layout. The contrast between the rough rockery, the smooth pond and the rectangular hall, vertical — horizontal — vertical, makes a pleasing scene for both those in the garden and those in the hall looking out into the garden. The gardens at either side of the hall are designed to harmonize with that in front. The entire design features the hall as the main motif of the total scene.

Alternatively, the main hall may, if there is an irregular but ample area before and around it, be sequestered. The Yuan Xiang Tang

Sectional and longitudinal section drawing, viewing northwards, of the courtyard of Hu Yuan Garden in Soochow.

(Far-Fragrant Hall) of Zhou Zheng Yuan Garden is an example of this classic layout. Xiang Xie (Fragrant Lotus-root Hall) in the Yi Yuan Garden and Han Bi Shan Fang (Conserve Green Mountain House) in the Liu Yuan Garden in Soochow are partly hidden among decorative hollow rocks, shrubs and flowers.

PAVILIONS

Pavilions were used to entertain intimate friends in an informal setting. In addition, they were a favorite place for members of the family to relax and enjoy the garden. Pavilions were commonly built with movable screen walls. These carved screen walls were removed in good weather so the occupants had no windows between them and the garden. Pavilions were of two kinds — a two- or three-story structure or a platform/loft set on pillars. In both cases the intent was to elevate the principal viewing floor above the shrubbery and low trees so viewers could look over and across the garden or pond. Pavilions were usually placed midway up a low lying hillside facing a water scene.

104 *The Garden Art of China*

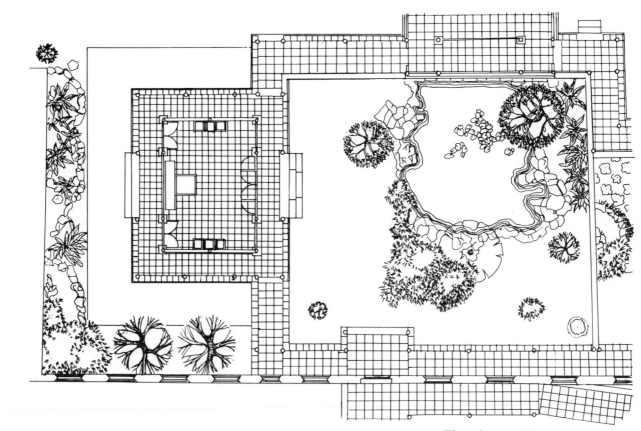

Plane figure of Ting Yu Xuan
(Rain-listening Hall) of Zhou
Zheng Yuan Garden in Soochow.

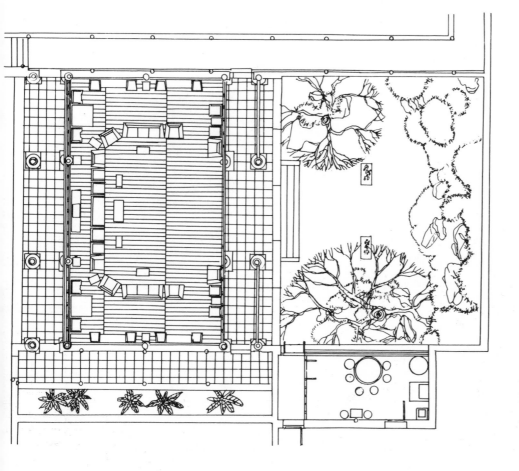

Plane figure of Yu Lan Tang
(Magnolia Hall) of Zhou Zheng
Yuan Garden in Soochow.

Access to the top or viewing floor was by an interior staircase or by steps built in a winding path through a rockery adjacent to the pavilion. Great care was taken that pavilions were built in a size and proportion suitable to the neighboring water surface to create a harmonious relation between the two features. Jian Shan Lou (Seeing Mountain Storey) of the Zhou Zheng Yuan Garden and Yan Cui Ge (Far Green Two-storied Pavilion) of Liu Yuan Garden in Soochow, provide excellent examples of harmonious proportions, carefully realized.

Pavilions, whether of the loft or multi-story type were built in the form of a square, polygon or round. In any case they must have windows on all sides which if local conditions permit may be removed.

The Xie (pavilion at waterside or terrace) and Fang (boat-shaped pavilion on water) are structures built on the edge of a pond or lake.

The latter always projects out into the water. Both structures serve the dual functions of a decorative feature as well as a place to rest and view the water features. Zhou Ying Shui Ge (Tasselwash Water Pavilion) in the Wang Si Yuan Garden is a fine example of Xie. The Fang is also called Han Chuan (Land Boat) and was built along the lines of the gaily-painted pleasure boats frequently used on large garden lakes. Probably the best example of Fang is the Marble Boat in the Summer Place of Beijing. It follows conventional boat construction with the bow, cabin and stern. Like the structure of a common boat it is a little lower in the middle with a two-story stern, high enough for viewing the surrounding water scenes. Other examples are the Xiany Zhou (Fragrant Islet) in the Zhou Zheng Yuan Garden and the Hua Feng Zhai (Painted Boat Room) in the Yi Yuan Garden in Soochow.

Sectional and longitudinal section drawing of Feng Xiang Lane's courtyard in Yangchow.

Waterside *Taxodium distichum*

A small bridge to Palm Garden

Cereus hexagonus

Plate 5

Ornamentals on window shelf

Nymphaea tetragona in small pond

Cactus plants in greenhouse

Plate 6

A pond scene viewed through a hole-window in Liu Yuan Garden, Soochow.

Furniture made of old vines, installed in Yuan Xiang Tang (Far Fragrant Hall) of Zhou Zheng Yuan Garden in Soochow.

Garden Architecture 107

Jinshan Hill (Coal Hill), a part of the Summer Palace, the highest elevation in Beijing.

Five-Dragon Pavilions in Bei Hai (North Sea) of Beijing.

Styles of Pavilions

In the Imperial gardens pavilions are insignificant and not particularly noteworthy in relation to the other magnificent buildings, but they are essential structures in private gardens and public scenic spots where they are used to beautify built-up mountain and water scenes. The following are the typical types and styles of pavilions seen in private Chinese gardens:

The triangle type. The triangle pavilion with a roof which tilts up and toward the apex was commonly built at the bend of a zigzag bridge to contrast with the rocks jutting up out of the water. Decorative climbers are usually grown on the sides away from the water. Such an embellishment greatly beautifies the waterscapes.

Square, hexagonal and octagonal pavilions. These pavilions, with a roofline rising to a common point and single eave, were the most traditional style and very common in both private gardens and at scenic spots. The roof-slopes of these pavilions are steep — about one-half the height of the pavilion columns. They are usually built on man-made "mountains", hills or rockeries partly hidden among green bushes. Their "nice" positions are advantageous for looking at far-off scenes.

The double-eave tip-roofed pavilion. This is a rich and magnificent pavilion not widely used in private gardens but common in the Imperial Gardens such as the Ba Jian Ting (Octagon Pavilion) in the Summer Palace of Beijing.

The ridge-roof pavilion. There are several types of the ridged-roof pavilion: 2-sided symmetrically-sloped, thin-topped type and retroflex. They may be rectangular, octagonal or fan-shaped. This type of pavilion was often built along a lakeside, on a terrace or at a bend in a gallery. Such pavilions are particularly fine places to rest and view the surrounding scenery.

Complex pavilion. The complex pavilion consists of two or more pavilions constructed as a single structure with common floor level. A particularly fine example is that on the ridge of Longevity Hill in the Summer Palace of Beijing, which consists of two identical hexagonal pavilions.

Half-pavilion. This structure is, as the name implies, only half a conventional pavilion built against a white wall and colourfully decorated. It is often linked to an open gallery or rockery at its left and right sides. In the garden scene it is made to look like a highly decorated pavilion.

The chapter dealing with pavilions and kiosks in the Chinese gardening book *Yuan Zhi* written by the artist and gardener Ji Cheng, provides the following advice for the proper use and siting of such structures. "Pavilions and kiosks are laid out in various styles according to natural local conditions, their sites are generally on mountain slopes or tops, near lakesides and creeks, and in large plantings of bamboo, shrubs and flowers. They serve as foils to landscapes and waterscapes."

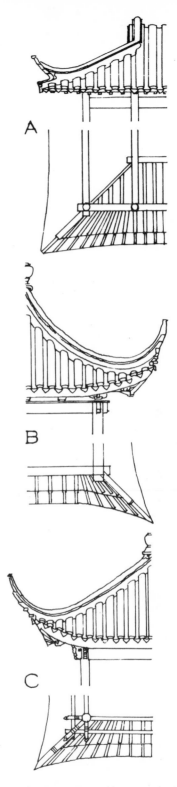

The angle structures of houses and pavilions in the classical gardens of Soochow:
A. Xiu Qi Ting (Beautifully Embroidered Pavilion) of Zhou Zheng Yuan Garden
B. Jin Li Ting (Golden Chestnut Pavilion) of Yi Yuan Garden (Happy Garden)
C. Lu Qi Ting (Green Pavilion) of Zhou Zheng Yuan Garden.

Sectional and longitudinal section
drawing, viewing westwards to Ting Yu
Xuan (Rain-listening Hall) of Zhou
Zheng Yuan Garden in Soochow.

Sectional and longitudinal section
drawing, viewing northwards to the
whole scene of Guan Yuan Fang
(Cloud-crowned-peak) of Liu Yuan
Garden in Soochow.

GALLERIES TO EMBELLISH THE GARDEN SCENE

In Chinese gardens, galleries provide the varied motifs necessary to establish the meaning of the garden and are intrinsically important scenic features. Galleries and corridors serve as ties between various architectural structures and to carry the viewer from one garden scene to the next in the sequence and order conceived by the garden artist. In addition, they provide a sheltered and comfortable means for the viewer to appreciate the constantly changing quality and beauty of the scenes as the seasons unfold and the weather changes from sunny to cloudy, clear to rainy and summer to fall and winter to spring.

In siting and designing a gallery it is necessary to construct the structure in keeping with local conditions. Ji Cheng said in his *Yuan Zhi* that "a gallery is built in accord with topographic conditions, it rises with the line of the hillside, bends and turns along the natural trend of the water's edge and with suitable and artistic treatment of its design, and colours to harmonize with the surrounding garden".

In the Liu Yuan Garden of Soochow there is a Bu Lang (passage gallery) which is of a classic pattern. It starts from the entrance porch, passes through the entire garden and terminates at the eastern boundary. It conducts the visitor in an orderly progress through the several scenes of which Liu Yuan Garden is composed so that its full magnificence and variety can be appreciated. In addition, the gallery is the essential element integrating the spatial relations of groups of buildings, the various garden scenes and the local topographical trends. It rises, falls, bends and turns the beautiful scenic areas of the garden. Its compact, elemental and rhythmic design is an artistic success.

The Bu Lang (Stroll Gallery) of Zhou Zheng Yuan Garden, in contrast, is laid out in a free style. It breaks and starts again in an intermittent sequence. It also serves to guide the progress of the visitor but instead of confining him to the view from the "outside", the breaks permit him to enter the garden scene. The visitor then not only views the scene from the "inside" — he becomes a part of the scene. This leads to a wonderful harmony with Nature. Bu Long is a remarkable artistic composition and a striking example of the unique and ingenious sensibilities incorporated in the classical gardens of Soochow.

The Siting of Galleries

Galleries are usually located in one of four kinds of site: Along the water edge, over water, midway up the slope of a hill or on the flat ground. Galleries are accordingly laid out in keeping with the differing requirements and functions demanded by the site.

Galleries built along the water edge. Galleries built alongside the water feature are called Shui Lang (Water Gallery). They function both as places for viewing waterscapes and to connect other structures on the water surface. Waterside galleries are carefully related to the water surface and the water edge in keeping with the specific environmental conditions presented by the specific site.

If the bank is clearly defined, gallery foundations are based on the bank wall and so are closely connected with the water. A nice pattern is the gallery of Hua Fang Zhai (Painted Boat-Room) of the North Sea Park in Beijing which is sited along the retaining wall of a square water feature. It functions as a link between the surrounding structures. Another pattern is the waterside gallery of Zhan Yuan (Sight-seeing Garden) of Nanking. It is based on the pond bank against the border wall. This waterside gallery provides a fine effect that not only relieves the narrow and monotonous pathway between the pond and the wall, but also enriches the overall garden composition as the element which unifies the rockery, other structures and the plantings of ornamental shrubs, bamboos and flowers.

If the contour of the water bank is irregular, the water gallery should follow its meandering line and coordinate other structures and bankside plantings. The design objective, in any case, should be to shape a garden based on the water scene.

Galleries built over water. Galleries are sometimes built over a water feature. As with waterside galleries, their functions are three-fold. First, they serve to connect pavilions, kiosks and island constructed in the water feature. Secondly, they provide the means to guide the visitor along and through the waterscape in the way conceived by the garden artist. And lastly they are designed to harmonize with the overall design of the waterscape and hence to embellish the scene. In some cases, the gallery is the garden element used to unify all the elements of the waterscape. Galleries built over the water may be constructed either on a continuous foundation or alternatively on piers much like a bridge. In the latter case the water can flow under the gallery as in the Wavy Gallery in the Zhou Zheng Yuan Garden of Soochow.

Galleries on a hillside or terrace. Galleries built on a hillside or terrace are called Pa Shuan Youlang (Gallery of Climbing Hills). As in the case of waterside galleries they function as a connection between structures and as places to rest and sightsee and enrich the beauty of the hill.

Hillside galleries are usually oriented in one of two ways. The first is a gallery which follows the contour of the hillside horizontally. Such galleries are connected with other structures by stone steps. The second type of gallery is vertically oriented and follows natural trails ascending the hill. Such galleries climb the hill in a zigzag undulating manner following the topographical trend, making the ascent convenient and easy for visitors to negotiate.

Needless to say, both types of structure are designed in keeping with the principle of maintaining the beautiful features of Nature but enhancing them through the ingenuity of the landscape artist.

Galleries on plane ground. Galleries built on plane ground presented a special challenge to landscape artists. Inasmuch as such galleries, particularly in private gardens, were used to connect the various buildings used as living quarters, space was at a premium. Therefore, the galleries had to be narrow and yet relate properly to the size of the buildings which they connect and against which (the single-sided gallery) they are situated. Because the topography changes but little within such a limited area, the gallery must be very compact. Meeting all of these constraints in an esthetically satisfying manner in a large number of gardens throughout China is one of the notable achievements of the Chinese gardening arts.

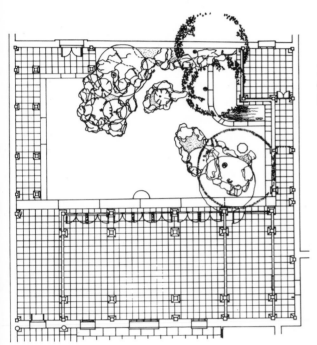

Plane figure of front courtyard of Feng Xian Hong (Bellows Lane) in Yangchow.

A square pavilion, Lu Yi Ting (Blue Ripples Pavilion), of Zhou Zheng Yuan Garden in Soochow.

General plane figure of Hai Tang Chun Wu (Begonia Flower-bed of Spring) of Zhou Zheng Yuan Garden in Soochow.

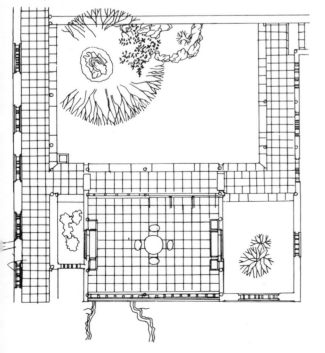

A

B

C

The Styles of Galleries

The several styles of galleries used in Chinese gardens include galleries with viewing windows on one or both sides, the lattice window gallery, the compound gallery and the 2-storied gallery.

The function of the gallery with viewing windows on both sides is to separate scenic areas having different garden features and objectives. Thus, the great gallery known as the Long Gallery of the Summer Palace of Beijing is more than 600 meters long and consists of 273 spacious rooms with open windows on both sides and is sited alongside the great Kunming Lake in front of Longevity Hill. The gallery is curved in a radial arc so that visitors can view the waterscape on one side and the mountain scenes on the other.

The gallery with windows on one side is most commonly used alongside residential buildings or on horizontal hillsides where it is cut into the hillside. In both cases, the visitor's view is directed only to a single scene.

The lattice window gallery is so named from the wooden lattice which may be installed or removed depending upon the weather. Lattice galleries are often used in private gardens, as are lattice pavilions.

The compound gallery is called Fu Lang. It is partitioned off by a wall with viewing windows in the middle. On either side of the gallery there are different scenes. Such a gallery is the curved Cang Lang Ting in the Zhou Zheng Yuan Garden with a waterscape on the north side and a landscape on the south. The gallery was curve-shaped, and thus the scene on both sides can be seen through the viewing windows.

The 2-storied gallery is called Fu Dao (double way). They are usually built at the foot of a hill along a waterside to guide the visitor from a scene at one elevation to the next scene at a higher elevation. The 2-storied gallery of the Summer Palace connects the waterscape to the fascinating wonders of the grottos in the built-up area alongside the lake.

Another example of the 2-storied gallery is on Qiong Hua Islet in the North Sea Park of Beijing, built alongside the foot of hill. The ground storey faces the water surface of the lake for viewing the waterscape, while the upper storey is used to view the mountain scenes afar.

The common trees seen in Chinese gardens:
A. weeping willows
B. maple, Chinese sweet gum (*Liquidambar taiwaniana*), Poplar
C. elm, Chinese wisteria (*Wistaria sinensis*)
D. pine.

D

BRIDGES

In Chinese gardening, bridges are used both to carry the visitor across a watercourse and to embellish the water scene and the gardens on both sides of the bridge.

The following general principles are used to guide the design of the bridge:

A bridge spanning a large lake or pond should be grand and magnificent in outward appearance when viewed as part of the entire water scene, but must be exquisite in all details when viewed close-up by the visitor.

A bridge spanning a stream or other narrow water feature is generally designed with simple and brisk outline in harmony with its environment. If it crosses a rushing current, suitable design calls for it to be placed well above the water and have high balustrades installed. However, if it crosses a placid water surface, the bridge is placed only slightly higher than the water level, and without balustrades.

If a water feature is constructed in relation to a hillside and bridges span creeks or inlets at the foot of the hill, they should be built on a low profile to provide contrast with the lofty and steep hill.

Bridges spanning placid water surfaces must be of a design which is beautiful both when seen by itself and as seen reflected in the mirror-like water.

Bridges connecting two flat areas in the garden should be built in a wavy contour to contrast with the flatness.

Bird's-eye view of Hai Tang Chun Wu (Begonia Flower-bed in Spring).

Indoor perspective in contrast to front courtyard scene of Wu Feng
Xian Guan (Five-peak Fairy Hall) in Liu Yuan Garden of Soochow.

The indoor furnitures and fixtures in the Lin Quan Qi Shi Zhi Guan
(Hall for Venerated People at the Forested Well).

116   *The Garden Art of China*

Various types of corridors in classical garden constructions of Soochow: A. Shi Zi Lin (Lion Grove)   B. Cong Long Ting (Blue-wave Pavilion)   C. Liu Yuan Garden   D. Zhou Zheng Yuan Garden   E. He Yuan Garden (Crane Garden)   F. Chang Yuan Garden (Garden-of-ease).

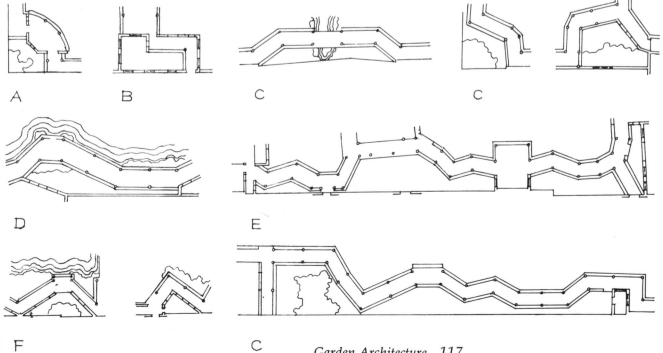

A   B   C   C

D   E

F   C

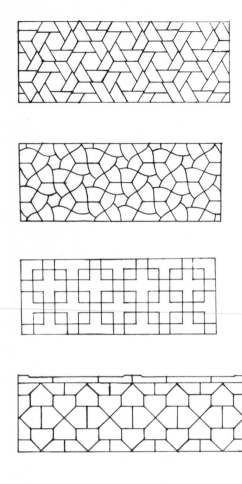

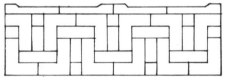

Five patterns of wooden banisters in Ji Cheng's gardening book *Yuan Zhi.*

Shapes of Bridges

The shapes of bridges in Chinese gardens are principally of four patterns: the flat bridge, the arch bridge, the pavilion bridge and the gallery bridge.

The flat bridge is simple and tidy in appearance. Depending upon the width of the water course to be crossed, three rectangular slabs of stone are used. The bridge surface connects with the path pavement at the same level. The only decorative treatment required is the placing of a large, handsome, natural-shaped rock at the side of each end to act as a marking guide for the viewer.

A zigzag flat bridge is made of a number of flat slabs of rock, with each course of slabs offset from the others and supported on natural rocks raised slightly from the water line as bridge piers. Such an arrangement makes the viewer feel as if he is walking on the water.

The arch bridge is grand and elegant. It is usually used to span a broad water surface such as the Shi Qi Kong Quao (17-hole Bridge) of seventeen arches in the Summer Palace of Beijing. It serves both as a bridge and as a foil for the waterscape. Its picturesque figure is an architectural high point in Chinese gardens and is greatly beloved by landscape artists.

The pavilion bridge is as the name implies — a bridge upon which one or more pavilions are built. In addition to providing a passage across a waterscape, the pavilions provide a serene setting for the viewer to stop, rest and appreciate the entire waterscape. Pavilion bridges are often seen in Chinese gardens because they greatly beautify large waterscapes. Pavilion bridges enhance a large flat waterscape by providing a contrasting vertical layered feeling in space. The Wu Ting Quio (Five pavilion Bridge) of Shou Si Hu in Yangchow is an excellent example.

The gallery bridge is not widely used in Chinese gardening, although it is one of the most distinctive structures used in Chinese classical garden design. A remarkable example can be seen in the Ji Chang Yuan Garden of Wusih. The gallery bridge is simply a gallery built across a water body. So it incorporates the characteristics of both a bridge and a gallery. Gallery bridges are, like pavilion bridges, built close to the water surface.

Elevation drawing at the north-side architectural construction of the Second-well of Hui Mountain in Wusih.

118   *The Garden Art of China*

Snow scene of the
Summer Palace,
Beijing.

Seventeen-arch
Bridge in Kunming
Lake, Summer Palace,
Beijing.

Temple of Heaven,
Summer Palace,
Beijing.

Wu Ting Qiao (Five-
Pavilion Bridge of
Shou Si Hu,
Yangchow.

Bird's-eye view of Hu Yuan Garden in Soochow.

COURTYARDS

In Chinese classical gardens, the courtyard is a mandatory composition designed to create multiple quiet environments through the creation of series of scenes. The true test of a Chinese garden designer is to be found in the ingenuity and esthetic sensitivity used to create the interrelated but separate environments of the courtyard garden.

In private residential gardens, courtyards are attached to the main residential buildings both in front and back of the main house. Each courtyard is an independent unit in space yet must link harmoniously with the other features of the garden. The following are the patterns of Chinese courtyards:

Sectional and longitudinal section drawing of Hai Tang Chun Wu (Begonia Flower-bed of Spring) of Zhou Zheng Yuan Garden, viewing northward.

A. In the Zhou Zheng Yuan Garden of Soochow, the eastern courtyard is a quadrangular area. It is divided by a long windowed gallery connecting the hall to the Hai Tang Chun Wu (Begonia Flower-bed of Spring). A curved gallery links to the western hall. Bananas have been planted on the south side of the gallery while a pond has been constructed on the north. Around the pond grow magnolias, sweet-scented osmanthus and bushes of bamboo. The scenes on both sides are endlessly fascinating as they change with the season.

Another pattern has been created in the courtyard in front of the Yu Lan Tang (Magnolia Hall) in the middle part of the same garden. The hall was the original residence. It is surrounded by a border wall on the south, east and west. Its central feature is a huge, aged magnolia tree full of fragrant flowers in spring. Peonies and bamboos are planted in the flowerbed made of lake rocks. The surrounding white border wall serves as a foil to this quiet and secluded place.

B. The Guan Yuan Fang (Cloud-crowned Peak) is the Liu Yuan Garden of Soochow and is built in front of the main hall, Yuan Yang Ting (Mandarin Duck Hall). The piled-up mountain is used to set off a small pond in which pygmy water lily (Nymphaes) is grown. The pond is positioned before this peak to embellish the courtyard scene. The piled-up hill is proportioned to harmonize with the dimensions of the scene and the surrounding architecture. To mitigate the sense of loneliness induced by a solitary peak, a hexagonal pavilion was built on the east side. Two lower peaks flank the main peak. The entire

Cymbidium ensifolium

Begonia rex-cultorum

Ornamentals on window shelf

Amaryllis reticulata var. *striatifolia*

Plate 7

Neottopteris nidus

Gymnosphaera podophylla

Codiaeum variegatum

Plate 8

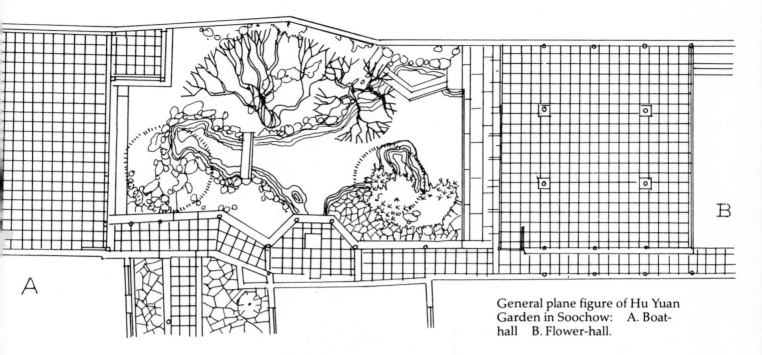

A

B

General plane figure of Hu Yuan Garden in Soochow: A. Boat-hall   B. Flower-hall.

mountain scene is planted with small shrubs and flowers to enhance the total view.

C. The courtyard of the Hu Yuan Garden of Soochow is small with a waterscape as its principal motif. The main focus of the scene is the irregularly shaped, curved pond, the sight lines of which lead the eye in multiple directions. Two slab bridges cross the water from south to north leading to a parlor above a half-pavilion. Despite the limited space, the cunning design of the pond and path make the water scene seem as if endless.

Along the pond-side several *Podocarpus macrophyllus*, *Chimonanthus praecox* and small bunches of bamboo are planted. The procession of plantings is interrupted by a few wonderful hollow rocks placed at irregular intervals. Thus, the picturesque scene is rich in lines and levels affording much food for thought.

D. The courtyard of the No. 2 Fountain in the World (Tian Xia Di Er Quan) of Hui Shan Mountain in Wusih is built along the foot of the mountain. A square pond is placed in front of the Yi Lan Tang (Rippling Water Hall) while the falls are located at the back of the building. The contrast between the vertical, irregular, active falls and the horizontal square quiet pond is strikingly beautiful and moving. A board on which are carved five big Chinese Characters *"Tian Xia Di Er Quan"* written by Emperor Qian Long of the Qing Dynasty when he went on an inspection tour there overhangs the building. The water from the fountain is famed for making excellent tea. The hall incorporates multiple levels of wavy lines, reminiscent of waves on water. The hall and contrasting water scenes provide a splendid and beautiful expression of water in its multifarious modes.

E. The courtyard of Feng Xian Hong (Bellows Lane) in Yangchow is sited in front of the parlor of a residence. Two short galleries extend from its east and west sides. The east gallery is connected with the backyard of the house, while the west gallery links to a half-pavilion in the south-west corner of the garden. A rockery facing the parlor is composed of lake rocks and culminates in a peak. The half-pavilion, supported on piers, stands over a pond as a water kiosk. Though the space available to compose this courtyard is far from spacious, its excellently balanced layout creates a placid, comfortable living and viewing scene. Plums, glossy privets, cypress, bamboos and flowering perennials are carefully and thoughtfully planted to make this scenic courtyard one of the loveliest and most attractive in China.

Sectional and longitudinal section drawing of the front courtyard of Feng Xian Hong (Bellow Lane) in Yangchow, viewing westward.

F. The Hu Pao Quan (Tiger-run Fountain) Courtyard of Hangchow is a raised level space with two vertical or sloping sides, higher to the north and lower to the south. The fountain is located in the middle between the two terraces. There is a small pond on the lower terrace to receive the water flowing from the fountain. Several lake rocks arise in the pond to decorate the water surface. Alongside the pond, ornamentals are planted. On the upper terrace, an open gallery Zhai Cui Xuan (Licking-greens Veranda) was built for viewing the surrounding scenes.

124   *The Garden Art of China*

OTHER GARDEN STRUCTURES

Walls, gates, doors, windows and paving used to organize garden space are some of the most ancient and constant elements in Chinese landscaping art. These universally employed garden structures contribute markedly to the unique appearance of Chinese gardens. They serve both as functional elements to achieve the design objective valued by the Chinese sense of esthetics — order, contrast, borrowing scenes, etc. — and as intrinsically decorative features of the garden. The extraordinary demands made upon such constructions for millenia have resulted in a number of fine traditional patterns which have proved their merit in solving garden design problems in a multitude of differing situations.

Garden Gateways

The entrance to nearly every Chinese classical garden is marked by an independent and self-contained structure — the garden gateway. These gateways are designed to form an intrinsically grand scene and to be appreciated on their own merits. The gateway is the central element in a scene commonly composed of artfully placed lake rocks, among which trees and flowers are planted to enrich and complete the scene.

The gateway of the Cang Lang Ting Garden of Soochow is one of the artistically most satisfying examples in China. It has been thoughtfully placed in a placid patch of water whose surrounding is embellished by carefully selected and planted trees, shrubs and flowers. The water seems to separate the garden into two parts, the outer and the inner. Actually the water surface is ingeniously utilized to link these two parts as an organic whole. This cunning use of the water feature is in marked contrast to the more traditional means of delimiting the garden from the public thoroughfare through the use of border walls. A zigzag bridge across the water leads the way to the gateway itself. Two huge Chinese scholar trees stand gracefully on either side of the entry way. A series of lattice windows mounted in

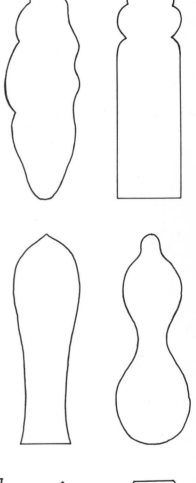

Twelve patterns of door type in Ji Cheng's gardening book *Yuan Zhi*.

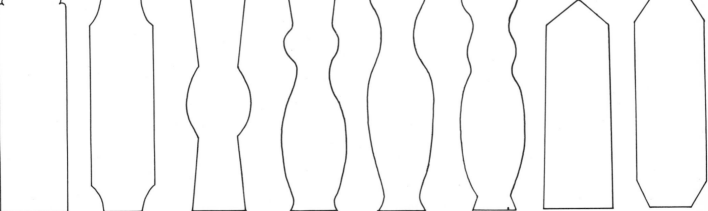

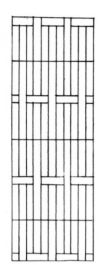

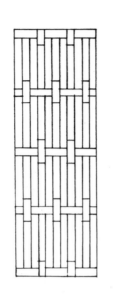

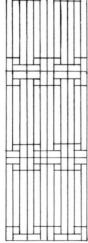

Five patterns of wooden windows in Ji Cheng's gardening book *Yuan Zhi*.

wooden frames fixed on a low yellow stone wall built along the water's edge protects the embankment.

This gateway typifies the best of the charming residential style in the region of rivers and lakes along the lower reaches of the Yangtse River — or for that matter in any area marked by abundant natural water features.

Doors

In classical Chinese gardens, distinct scenic areas are created, each having one principal feature which determines the design of the balance of the area. Thus piled-up mountains, water, buildings, etc. each delineate and determine a specific scene. Each unique scenic area is commonly separated from others by means of a border wall but joined by doorways in the wall. The door apertures in the border wall, as well as the shapes and styles of the wall doors are greatly varied and are based on the features of the specific site and the requirements imposed by the overall composition of the garden.

The design of door openings pose problems as great as designing a garden gate for they must be ingenious and exquisite in style within the constrained space available. They must be neat and compact yet embellish a simple and clear white wall. To maintain a harmonious transition between such simple structures and the scenes on either side the doorways should be decorated with a few beautiful hollow rocks, and plantings of trees and flowers arranged to form variant scenes in the manner of flower paintings. Walls function not only to serve as enclosing frames, but also to provide backgrounds and settings for certain sections of gardens — particularly to frame views to be seen through the openings.

In his book *Yuan Zhi* Ji Cheng recommends a variety of door shapes — full moon, sickle moon, flower vase, water chestnut, Ruyi (a decorative object, symbol of good luck) octagonal, hexagonal, plum flower, begonia, lotus petal, shell, hulu (bottle gourd), etc. All have been extensively used in Chinese gardens. But this master's work has been only a springboard for the creative imagination of countless landscape artists who have designed a multitude of ingenious doorways and doors.

Windows

Borrowing scenes through window apertures is a unique feature in Chinese classical gardens. In boundary walls, window apertures not only enrich the architectural charm of the wall, but also provide the means for instant and evocative contrasts between scenes and intensify the visual perception of the garden scenes viewed through them. A series of window apertures are, in the Chinese mind, likened to a series of vivid pictures.

Two types of window apertures are used: Kong Chuang (without paper or glass panes) and Lou Chuang (with paper or glass panes). They are constructed in a variety of shapes — square, horizontal rectangle, perpendicular rectangle, hexagon, circular, fan, leaf, etc., and decorated in many styles. The aperture without panes is also called

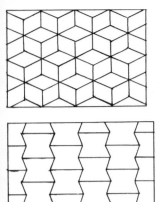 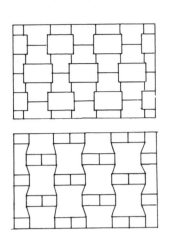  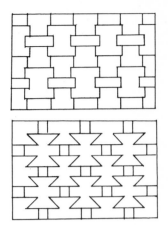

Yue Dong (moon windows). Moon windows placed in building walls provide ventilation and lighting in addition to their use as Hua Kuong (pictorial frames).

Walls

As mentioned earlier walls play an important role in the art of Chinese gardens: dividing the garden space into separate scenes; as foils to garden scenes; blocking the line of sight from outside the wall to provide contrast between and surprise in adjoining scenes; provide privacy. In addition, they are used as monumental or accent features to link and provide contrast with other architectural elements of the garden. The contrasting quality is designed to throw into relief the special architectural features both of the walls and the garden pavilions and galleries. The walls between hill scenes, water scenes, architectural elements, and various plantings of trees and flowers can,when designed in the context of harmony with Nature, be used to achieve effects of contrast or uniformity. They always organize independent and variegated courts and scenes in a natural manner.

Pavings

A subtle and little understood element in Chinese decorative garden architecture is the paving of paths outdoors and the continuation of this decorative paving indoors conceived of as integrated artistic features.

Paths can be made of brick, tile, chinaware or shingle stone chips stamped into well-prepared ground. Thus, decorative paths and paving not only make use of waste materials, but also enrich and harmonize with surrounding landscapes. When shingle is used, patterns are made through the use of stone of varied color. When bricks only are used, ornamental figures are produced by placing some bricks on edge to form geometrical patterns. Small square bricks can be used around flowerbeds to create a pattern of cracked ice.

Indoor paving is generally more decorative and of either more refined geometrical shapes including chequer, interwoven in sixes, linked hexagons and spiral whorls, or the naturalistic shapes of flowers, leaves, and fruits, and carpet-like patterns. Despite the increased ornamentation used in interior paving, it must be designed in the context of the paving used in the garden and treated as a part of the total garden scene.

The patterns of leaky-windows in Ji Cheng's gardening book *Yuan Zhi*.

Four patterns of floor tile paved by side-bricks in Ji Cheng's gardening book *Yuan Zhi*.

Garden Architecture 127

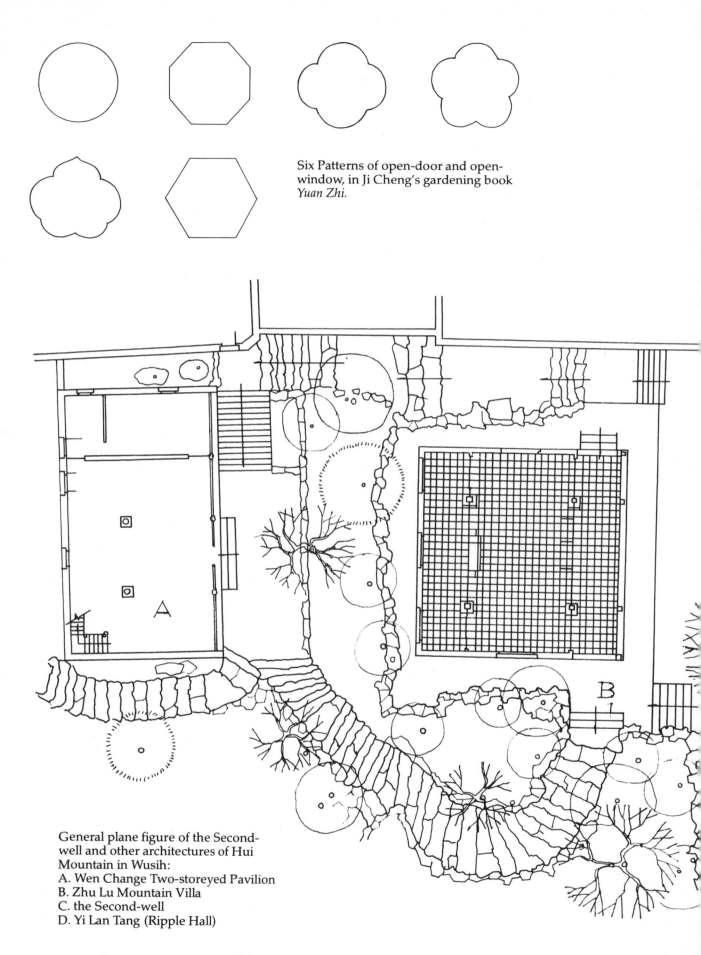

Six Patterns of open-door and open-window, in Ji Cheng's gardening book *Yuan Zhi*.

General plane figure of the Second-well and other architectures of Hui Mountain in Wusih:
A. Wen Change Two-storeyed Pavilion
B. Zhu Lu Mountain Villa
C. the Second-well
D. Yi Lan Tang (Ripple Hall)

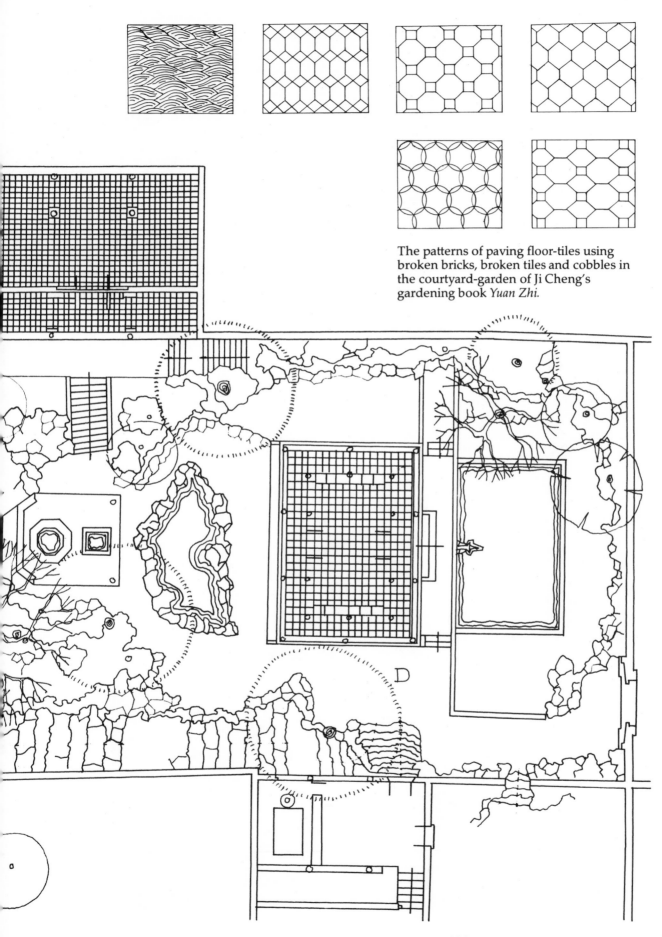

The patterns of paving floor-tiles using broken bricks, broken tiles and cobbles in the courtyard-garden of Ji Cheng's gardening book *Yuan Zhi*.

A full moon doorway in a classical garden in Soochow.

A crabapple-shaped doorway in Zhou Zheng Yuan Garden in Soochow.

Rockery and a small pond in Yu Yuan Garden in Shanghai.

Lungchiang (Dragon Wall) of Yu Yuan Garden.

Ming Xuan of Wang Shi Yuan Garden.

Interior of Ming Xuan in Wang Shi Yuan Garden.

COLOUR

In the imperial palace gardens of North China, attention is drawn to the massive structures through the application of vivid and striking colour. The common colour scheme employs red for columns, green roof tiles, and gold decoration against stark white walls. The imperial garden artists emphasized the central place of man-made structures in the garden scenes by drawing the viewer's attention to them through the use of brilliant colour and magnificent decoration.

On the other hand the artists creating private residential gardens along the lower reaches of the Yangtse River favoured lower and less dominant architectural styles and subdued colour to evoke a more serene quality. Chestnut brown roof beams, pillars and column heads which contrast with flat white are the norm. The garden artists endeavored to balance the role and perceptual sense of garden structures with that of mountains, ponds, and plantings. Their objective was to create an atmosphere which replicates the feelings induced by wilderness and the harmony to be found in Nature.

Indoor Fixtures and Furnishings

The canon of the Chinese gardening arts views the interior of buildings as an integral part of the garden design and esthetic. To the Chinese mind the walls of a building do not represent a discontinuity in the garden space but rather an intrinsic and integral element of the global concept of the garden. The same criteria of esthetic judgement and taste invoked in the creation of the garden apply to furnishings and fixtures used in the building.

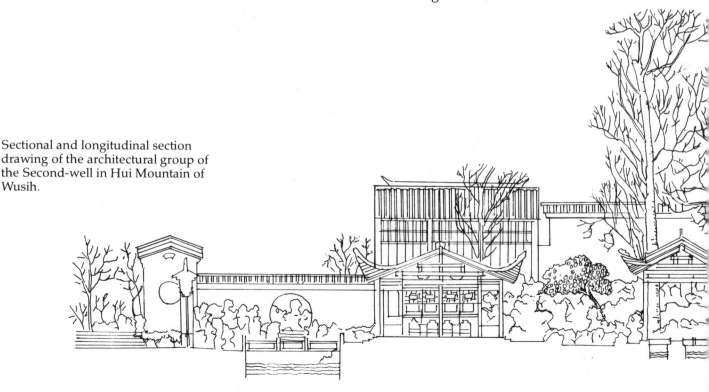

Sectional and longitudinal section drawing of the architectural group of the Second-well in Hui Mountain of Wusih.

Indeed, as has, I hope, been evident in the preceding discussion of garden architecture, the various types of structures built and their inherent design principles turn not on formal canons of architecture, but rather on their utility in viewing the garden and the provision of comfortable and easily used spaces within the context of the garden. Further, the design precepts guilding the artist are those which provide contrast to or harmony with the order inherent in Nature, as replicated in the varied garden scenes created.

Garden views change as the viewer in the house moves from one wall opening to another and from one room to the next. In addition the varied styles and decoration of doors, windows, window lattices, hanging scrolls, long windows and carvings greatly enrich the garden scenes just as frames focus and enrich a painting. Moreover, the doors and windows can be removed at will to change a confined and focused view to a more spacious and diffuse one.

The furniture with which a building is fitted is a component part of the indoor decoration used in Chinese gardens. Whether long, narrow, square or circular tables, with their accompanying chairs and stools, the design and materials used — red wood, rattan, or the twisted roots of banyan chosen for their wonderful shapes — all are selected and designed to fit coherently with the design of the garden.

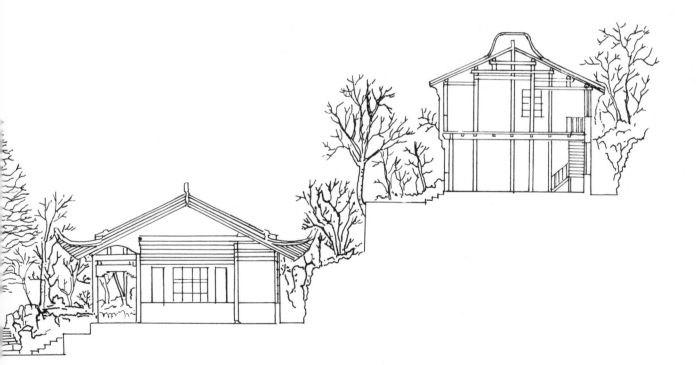

The articles and objects displayed in buildings are selected to harmonize or contrast with the tone set by the garden. Chinaware, jade, and marble carvings together with a number of living potted, miniature landscapes of tree and rock (Penjing) are the most commonly used. Objects hanging on the walls and columns — horizontal inscribed boards, poems, calligraphy, paintings, scrolls and screens — all are selected and placed in keeping with the esthetic intentions of the total environment. The many horizontal inscribed boards are a simplified introduction to the garden views. The calligraphy used is itself a masterpiece of the arts. In short, all the arts combine with the art of gardening to provide an integrated, coherent scene embodying the esthetic unity of Nature.

Sectional and longitudinal section drawing of Yu Lan Tang (Magnolia Hall) Courtyard of Zhou Zheng Yuan Garden, viewing westward.

8 Design Principle for Planting Trees and Flowers

The thoughtful and careful design of the plantings of trees and flowers is critical to the successful execution of the art of gardens in China. The correct and aesthetically sound selection and siting of plants not only creates the views for which the structural planning, design and work related in the preceding chapters is oriented but also is the element which brings the total conception to life and completes the cultural and symbolic significance of the garden. The plantings harmonize all the motifs of the landscape to create a dynamic, living microcosm of nature and symbolize the eternal harmony of the universe.

ARTISTIC CONCEPTION OF PLANTS

The utilization of trees and flowers in Chinese gardens replicates the principles and applications of the art of gardens embodied in the landscape, waterscape layout. The objective is replication of the underlying forms and functions of the Natural Order revealed in mountains-and-waters-and-forests in both tangible and metaphysical terms. Moreover, the selection, siting and culture of the plant materials is intimately related to the art of Chinese painting linked through shared views and expression of the fundamental truth of the universe. From the artistic as well as botanic points of view the artist and creator of Chinese classical gardens is deeply concerned with the habitats, shapes, colours, the appearance of leaves, flowers, branches, stems and trunks of the plants. In addition to the qualities and characteristics of each species the landscape artist is preoccupied by the interrelationships between species; between plants and the habitat; and most importantly between plants in their natural habitats and man. The proper relationship between all these elements reflects the natural law

The entrance of Yi Yuan Garden in Soochow.

135

and ethical order of the Universe. Classical Chinese poets and writers developed well-defined and clear views of the status and relationships obtained between plants, habitats, mankind and the Natural Order.

THE SPECIES USUALLY USED IN CHINESE GARDENS

In Chinese gardens, native plants are cultivated to reveal the unique features of each locality. As a consequence, and save for some imperial gardens in which the intent is to make a botanic garden reflecting the floral diversity of the world, Chinese garden artists employ native plants and site specific forms of traditional plants symbolically important to Chinese culture.

Due to the near universal admiration of Chinese gardens, the most commonly used trees and shrubs are well-known throughout the world. They include pine, bamboo, plum, sweet-scented osmanthus, gingko, camellia, weeping willow, wintersweet, begonia, magnolia, peony, Chinese wisteria, and azalea. The herbaceous and flowering plants include chrysanthemum, the orchids, narcissus, lotus, etc. In their history of cultivation for more than 3,000 years hundreds of varieties and cultivars have been developed from each of these species.

Chinese orchids are traditionally called the Xiang Zu (the ancestor of fragrance). They are typically cultivated in pots for decorative use indoors as well as outdoors in shade houses for their beautiful leaves and fragrant flowers. Narcissus is planted in beds out-of-doors but is also grown in pots or glazed earthen basins filled with pebbles and water as an indoor ornamental. The lotus is cultivated in ponds or basins not only for its fragrant and beautiful flowers but for its leaves for medicinal use, its seeds and roots as delicious edibles, and its symbolic use as a sign of purity.

In Chinese garden practice, plants are classified in keeping with their characteristics and landscaping and economic value as follows:

Grove and shade trees are fundamental plants to form horizontal and vertical layers in the landscape space. They are essential to sound garden design.

EVERGREEN CONIFEROUS TREES

Cedrus deodara	deodar cedar
Chamaecyparis obtosa	hinoki cedar
Cryptomeria fortunei	cryptomeria
Pinus aspera	brocaded pine
Pinus bungeana	lacebark pine
Pinus densiflora	Japanese red pine
Pinus parviflora	Japanese white pine
Pinus pinaster	cluster pine
Pinus taiwanensis	Taiwan pine
Pinus thunbergii	Japanese black pine
Platycladus orientalis	oriental arborvitae
Podocarpus macrophyllus	yew podocarpus

<pre>
           DECIDUOUS CONIFEROUS TREES
Metasequoia glyptostroboides   Chinese redwood
Pseudolarix kaempferi   golden larch
Taxodium ascendens   pond cypress
Taxodium distichum   bald cypress

           EVERGREEN BROAD-LEAVED TREES
Cinnamomum camphora   camphor tree
Eucalyptus robusta   gum tree
Ficus retusa   banyan

           DECIDUOUS BROAD-LEAVED TREES
Firmiana simplex   Chinese parasol
Sophora japonica   Chinese scholartree
Liquidambar formosana   Chinese sweet gum
Quercus acutissima   Sawtooth oak
Ulmus parvifolia   Chinese elm
Salix babylonica   Weeping willow
Populus tomentosa   Chinese white poplar
</pre>

Flowering trees and shrubs are planted for their attractive habit, various colours and pleasant fragrance. They are also important component parts of garden views both structurally and as specimens.

<pre>
                   EVERGREENS
Camellia japonica   camellia
Daphne odora   winter daphne
Eupatorium chinensis   baby chrysanthemum
Gardenia jasminoides   cape jasmine
Magnolia grandiflora   bull bay
Nerium indicum   sweet-scented oleander
Osmanthus fragrans   sweet-scented osmanthus
Rhododendron simsii   azalea
</pre>

Osmanthus trees planted in the courtyard of Gui Xuan (Osmanthus Hall) of Wang Shi Yuan Garden in Soochow.

Design Principle for Planting Trees and Flowers 137

Cercis chinensis	Chinese redbud
Chimonanthus praecox	wintersweet
Hibiscus mutabilis	Chinese hibiscus
Hibiscus syriacus	Rose of Sharon
Hydrangea macrophylla	big-leaf hydrangea
Jasminum nudiflorum	winter jasmine
Lagerstroemia indica	crape myrtle
Prunus mume	plum
Punica granatum	pomegranate
Rosa chinensis	Chinese rose
Syringa oblata	broad-leaved lilac

Fruit trees are planted both as ornamentals for their attractive shape, colour and fragrance in all four seasons and also for their economic value in providing fruit and important medicinals.

EVERGREENS

Citrus medica	citron
Citrus sinensis	tangerine
Eriobotrya japonica	loquat
Fortunella margarita	kumquat
Ilex cornuta	Chinese holly
Myrica rubra	red bayberry
Nandina domestica	nandina

DECIDUOUS

Chaenomeles sinensis	Chinese flowering crabapple
Diospyros kaki	persimmon
Prunus salicina	apricot plum
Prunus persica	peach
Punica granatum	pomegranate
Pyrus pyrifolia	peach
Ziziphus jujuba	date

Leafy trees are used as ornamentals for their charm, habit, colour and willingness to grow in dense groupings.

EVERGREENS

Aucuba japonica	Japanese aucuba
Buxus sempervirens	Chinese littleleaf box
Fatsia japonica	Japanese aralia
Ilex cornuta	Chinese ilex
Ligustrum lucidum	glossy privet
Musa paradisiaca	banana
Rhapis excelsa	palm

DECIDUOUS

Acer mono	painted maple
Gingko biloba	gingko
Liquidambar taiwaniana	Chinese sweet gum
Sapium sebiferum	Chinese tallow tree

Chinese wisteria (*Wisteria sinensis*) in Zhou Zheng Yuan Garden, Soochow.

138   *The Garden Art of China*

Echinocactus grusonii

Cactus plants in greenhouse

Canna indica

Plate 9

Guesthouse Garden scene

Cycas revoluta

Guesthouse Garden scene

Plate 10

Populus tomentosa	Chinese white poplar
Salix babylonica	Weeping willow

Vines and climbers are used as foils against rocks, fences, flower frames and walls to make the surrounding scenery more picturesque and natural.

EVERGREENS

Antigonon leptopus	coral vine
Catharanthus roseus	madagascar periwinkle
Jasminum mesnyi	primrose jasmine
Jasminum nudiflorum	winter jasmine
Lonicera japonica	trumpet honeysuckle
Trachelospermum jasminoides	white-flower vine

DECIDUOUS

Campsis grandiflora	Chinese trumpet creeper
Cuamoclit pennata	cypress vine
Parthenocissus tricuspidata	Japanese ivy
Rosa banksiae	bank's rose
Vitis vinifera	white grape
Wisteria sinensis	Chinese wisteria

Bamboos occupy a place of special affection, esteem and regard in Chinese culture. They are viewed as representative of the noblest virtues in mankind. They are consequently widely planted for both symbolic and ornamental purposes.

Arundinaria amabilis
Arundinaria pseudo-ambilis
Bambusa textilis
Bambusa ventricosa
Chimonobambusa quadrangularis
Indocalamus nanunicus
Lingnania chungii
Nipponocalamus fortunei
Phyllostachys bambusoides
Sinobambusa intermedia
Sinobambusa ssp

A large crape myrtle tree on the rockery in Guan Zhu Shang Zhung (Beautiful Surrounding Mountain Villa), Soochow.

Herbaceous flowering plants are used to provide colour and foreground material in ornamental gardens. Some are also grown for economic value in Chinese medicine.

Aster tataricus	Tatarian aster
Callistephus chinensis	China aster
Camellia japonica	common camellia
Chimonanthus praecox	wintersweet
Cymbidium kanran	winter cymbidium
Cymbidium sinensis	dark-purple cymbidium
Dahlia pinnata	common dahlia
Dendranthema morifolium	Chinese chrysanthemum

Dianthus caryophyllus	carnation
Gladiolus gandavensis	gladiolus
Narcissus tazetta 'Orientalis'	polyanthus narcissus
Nelumbo nucifera	lotus
Paeonia suffruticosa	peony
Prunus mume	Japanese apricot
Rhododendron pulchrum	lovely rhododendron
Rosa chinensis	China rose

Several Chinese methods of drawing trees:
A. two trees separated
B. two trees intersected
C. three trees in drawing
D. five trees in drawing.

A

B

THE ART OF CONCERTED PLANTING OF TREES AND FLOWERS

The art of concerted planting is closely linked to the canons of traditional Chinese brush painting. The landscape artist aims to achieve the twin objective of framing each individual plant to display its natural habit and colour while harmoniously integrating the line and colour of the entire scene in accord with the canons of painting. The viewer must be able to see both the natural beauty of the plants, their figure and colours, and the harmony of poetic and artistic lines in the scene. These objectives must be realized by the artist so that to the viewer the scene seems effortless and natural. The successful achievement of these objectives requires great creative insight and effort equal to that employed in a successfully realized painting, poem or piece of calligraphy.

The layout of plants in Chinese classical gardens is adapted from and related to the paintings of plants and flowers in traditional styles. This amalgamation of art forms — gardening and brush drawings — should be no surprise to the attentive reader. We have tried to stress the intimate relation of the high cultural arts and, in turn, the relation of art to the Natural Order and Chinese metaphysical views. Centuries-long careful observation by talented gardeners and artists led to a thorough and firm understanding not only of the habitat of plants but also how lovely and vividly they appear when healthy and vital in their natural settings. To remind the viewer of the beauty and natural fitness of plants in their native environment the same standards of judgement and criterion were invoked in criticizing the composition of both gardens and brush drawings — rich in contrast, habit, size, colour and liveliness.

In the classical gardens of Soochow, visitors will quickly notice that the trees and flowers are thriving in conditions carefully contrived to simulate their native conditions. The cold-resistant plants such as glossy privet, nandina, begonia, bamboo are living in the shade of walls. Camellia, bull bay, Japanese aucuba, Japanese aralia, Chinese flowering apple are growing on the sunny side of the wall or at the corner of the galleries in harmony with warmth-loving shrubs. Slender bamboos among a few scattered wonderful rocks occupy a lawn. Along the rocky gullies, pines and cypresses are standing firmly. In crevices of the rocks, ephiphytes such as *Victaria elogata* and *V. modesta* are flourishing. Along the lakeside, creek embankments, and low lying spots, *Metasequoia, Lythrum salicaria,* weeping willow and reed grow magnificently. All the plants are growing very well in favourable habitats suited to their needs and display their charm and beauty thanks to a centuries-old tradition of artistic composition and horticultural understanding.

The Chinese classical garden is an organic whole. The skeleton is provided by buildings and structures of unique architectural style, piled-up hills, waterscapes, scenes of various sizes and types and the ornamental paving of the paths, etc. The skeleton is carefully planned and executed to provide a fitting setting both in accord with the charm, habit, fragrance and colour of the plants and with the highly developed sense of the artistic and philosophical meaning of the Natural Order which is so marked and constant a feature of the Chinese cultural tradition.

Chinese poets, writers, artists and gardeners have endeavored to make concrete the unique artistic and poetic conception of Nature in Chinese classical culture. This conception recognized and clung to eternal verities and constants of the Natural Order of the world, which has led some observers to view the Chinese tradition as static and rigid. But such observations fail to take into account the equally profoundly held views of the role of time, in all its guises — the cycle of the day and the seasons; the extent of a lifetime with all its periods from birth to death; the rise and decline of the dynasties of the Chinese realm, etc. Other examples of the dynamism inherent in the Natural Order are familiar to students of Chinese culture and philosophy.

Artists, and in particular garden artists, endeavored to reflect this universal dynamism in Nature in the composition of the traditional Chinese garden. Thus in selecting and siting the traditional palate of plants the garden artist carefully considered and planted so that the composition reflected the harmonious variation as successful with the movement from dawn till dusk; from Spring to Winter through the seasons of the year. Even the changing weather, sunny or cloudy, rainy or snowy are comprehended in their compositional concepts.

In the classical gardens of Soochow, the selection and layout of plants followed traditional meanings associated with the four seasons: Spring, Summer, Autumn and Winter. Typical, but exceptionally well executed, is the Zhou Zheng Yuan Garden's Hai Tang Chun Wu (Begonias Flower-bed of Spring) which shows a variety of begonias in Spring time, a grove of crape myrtle rampant with purple flowers to symbolize the coming of the warm Summer months. Autumn is marked by the bright red leaves covering the hill in the west part of the Garden and a stand of camellias lends warmth and colour in the cold Winter months.

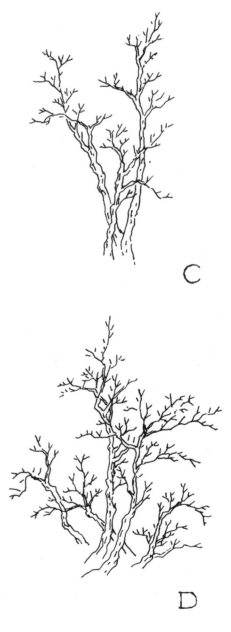

C

D

Design Principle for Planting Trees and Flowers **141**

The 12 Key Ornamentals Used in Nearly Every Chinese Garden

SPRING FLOWER

Cymbidium sinense	dark-purple cymbidium
Narcissus tazetta orientalis	Polyanthus narcissus
Paeonia suffruticosa	tree peony
Prunus mume	Japanese apricot

SUMMER FLOWER

Dianthus chinensis	Chinese pink
Gladiolus gardavensis	gladiolus
Rosa chinensis	China rose

AUTUMN FLOWER

Nelumbo nucifera	Chinese water-lily

WINTER FLOWER

Camellia reticulata	net-veined camellia
Chimonanthus praecox	wintersweet
Dendranthema morifolium	Chinese chrysanthemum
Rhododendron mucronatum	snow azalea

The 4 traditional spring plants each has its symbolic meaning. *Paeonia suffruticosa* symbolizes riches and honour in its large flowers which bloom in a riot of colour especially in the palace garden, where they were carefully cultivated and a number of hybrids and cultivars produced through thousands of years in practice. *Prunus mume*, which blooms luxuriantly in cold weather, symbolizes "strong-willed and noble-minded". *Cymbidium sinense* was famed as the "ancestor of fragrance" for its delicate odour in addition to its attractive leaves and flowers. *Narcissus tazetta* var. orientalis is described as "fairy girls riding the waves" for its fairy-like flowers in clusters among beautiful green leaves.

The traditional flowers of summer also have their symbolic associations. *Rosa chinensis* blooms profusely — its brilliant colour dominates the flower garden. It means everblooming. *Gladiolus gardavensis* is unique in the vast range of flower colour derived from the large number of cultivars. It means as beautiful as ten varieties of brocade. *Dianthus chinensis* is the best ornamental used to beautify rock gardens.

The traditional fall flower *Nelumbo nucifera* symbolizes purity. It grows "spotlessly white out of the mud and is not stained by the things of this world."

Camellias and rhododendrons are used to decorate the sides of piled-up mountains. They symbolize the season and mountain scenes in spring time. *Dendranthemas* is described as the "yellow plum" for its attractive colour and sweet odour. It symbolizes lustre and splendour.

Besides the 12 traditional key plants, bamboo is also highly valued in Chinese gardens. China is rich in species of bamboo. It is a great natural resource widely used in construction, agriculture, tools, basketry, as a food, works of art, etc. In addition to its economic

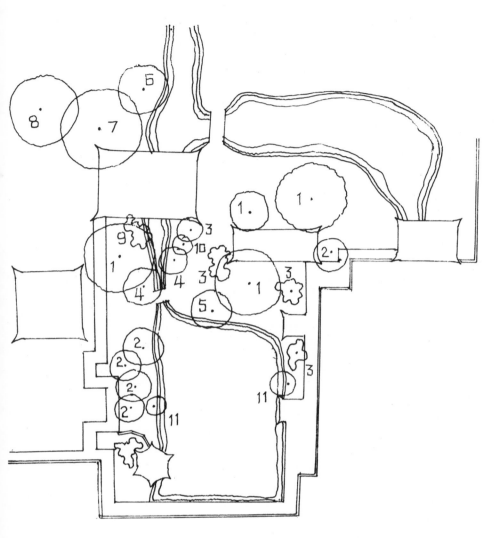

The planted spots of Zui Bai Pond-garden (there are many fragrant 100-year-old camphor trees) at Song Jiang near Shanghai:
1. *Cinnamomum camphora*
2. *Ligustrum lucidum*
3. *Musa nana*
4. *Punica granatum*
5. *Sophora japonica*
6. *Firmiana simplex*
7. Walnut tree
8. Elm tree
9. Nandina tree
10. Osmanthus tree
11. Crape myrtle

value, bamboo is one of the traditional materials used in landscaping. Around villages, in scenic areas, and along riversides and in gardens, they occupy a prominent place in the landscape.

Arundo donax (giant-reed), *Bambusa multiplex* (hedge bamboo), *Bambusa ventricosa* (buddha bamboo), *P. bambusoides* (Japanese timber bamboo), *Phyllostachys nigra* (black bamboo), *P. pubescens* (moso bamboo), *Pleioblastus augustifolius* (Japanese dwarf striped sasa bamboo), etc., are commonly used in gardening and landscaping as ornamentals, hedges, or for unique qualities being sought — for example, the buddha bamboo. Occasionally entire gardens are created using a variety of species.

Bamboo is symbolically important as one of the "three friends". The three friends are bamboo, pine, and plum. They do not wither in winter and so symbolize the virtuous person whose fortitude and uprightness are best revealed in time of trouble or when the going is rough.

Design Principle for Planting Trees and Flowers   **143**

THE BASIC METHOD OF CONCERTED PLANTING

In Chinese gardens and scenic spots, the first and most important principle is to plant trees, shrubs and herbaceous plants in an irregular way as they are in Nature. The grouping of plants must be made to appear completely natural by means of the subtle sense of arrangement developed through careful attention to both the plant associations and relationships found in Nature and the traditional canons of Chinese art.

Thus, in the confined space of a courtyard, a solitary tree will fully display its beautiful figure and colour, while larger spaces are laid out in several groups of the same species, or mixed with other species. The arrangement chosen is varied in keeping with local conditions and requirements. For example, evergreen trees match evergreen shrubs, or evergreen shrubs contrast with deciduous trees, or evergreen trees contrast with deciduous trees. These forms of planting are based on the esthetic objective of displaying the beauty of the entire group.

A classic example of well-planned and executed concerted plantings is found in the Zhou Zheng Yuan Garden. The Pipa Yuan (Loquat Garden) is composed entirely of loquat trees. In the west part of the garden a few Chinese sweet gums planted in a stand of pines create an attractive scene of "a bright red on the green". In the middle part (Zhong Yuan) of the garden the interweaving of weeping willows and peaches alongside the lake embankment are used to create yet a third beautiful scene. Pines are mingled with bamboos in the gully. Peaches and plums are mixed in the front and back courtyards to make varied views of marked contrast. Each of the several scenes is planned and executed to make a natural and integrated whole and then concerted to create a harmonious garden in complimentary or contrasting scenes.

The Natural Style for Grouping of Trees and Shrubs

A group of two of the same species but of different heights. The lower one is placed either before or behind the taller, but in the same line as the viewer will first see them. The trees should be planted so the top of the crown of the lowest reaches into the bottom of the crown of the highest.

A group of three of the same species stand side by side like a row of flying wild geese. They should be of different heights with the tallest placed in the middle.

A group of four divided into two pairs with one of each pair large and the other small. Alternatively, plant four all of different sizes, but the three larger embrace the smallest.

A group of five, all of the same species but of different heights with the two taller in the center, while the lower stand to the left and right but not in a line. Their crowns should be skillfully treated so as to present a scattered outline yet nicely crisscrossed with one another. When the number of plants exceeds five, modules of the above arrangements should be followed.

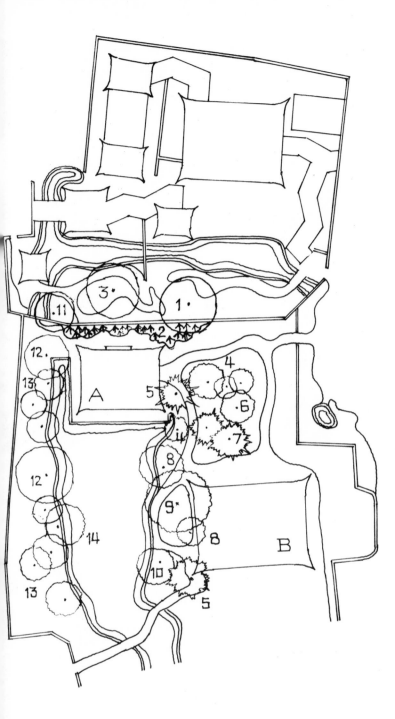

Trees planted near the Jiu Shi Xuan (Nine-lions Veranda) and De Yu Lou (Moon-gaining Storey) with the huge *Pterocarya stenoptera* as background, to enlarge spatial perception. The foreground consists of trees planted alongside both the embankments to increase the depth of field:

1. *Pterocarya stenoptera*
2. Bamboos
3. *Firmiana simplex*
4. *Ficus carica*
5. *Podocarpus macrophylla*
6. *Liquidambar formosana*
7. *Pinus thunbergii*
8. *Punica granatum*
9. *Cinnamomum*
10. *Erythrina indica*
11. *Ligustrum lucidum*
12. Wintersweet
13. *Metasequoia glyptostroboides*
14. *Salix babylonica*.

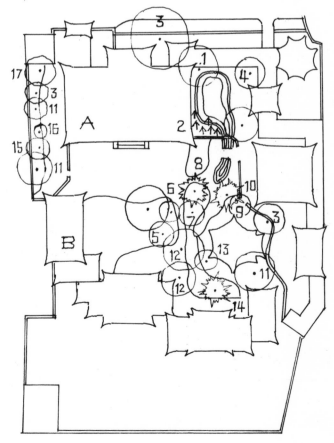

Garden scene of Cang Lang Ting (Blue Wave Pavilion), Zhou Zheng Yuan Garden, Soochow.

Peony planted in front of Yuan Xiang Tang (Far Fragrance Hall) of Zhou Zheng Yuan Garden.

Crape myrtle in Yi Yuan Garden, Soochow.

Middle garden scene of Liu Yuan Garden, Soochow.

Hemerocallis fulva planted beside a rock in Zhou Zheng Yuan Garden.

Indocalamus tessellatus on rockery of Cang Lang Ting.

Aucuba chinensis among rockery in Yi Yuan Garden.

Chinese trumpet creeper (Campsis grandiflora) in Shi Zi Lin (Lion Grove Garden), Soochow.

Design Principle for Planting Trees and Flowers 147

CREATION OF NATURAL LANDSCAPES

In landscape design, trees are the primary plant. Elements used in the composition of scenes based on the underlying structure of buildings, mountains and water. Their figure, colour and fragrance are considered to be the essential link between the underlying structure and the other plantings in the landscape. Their seasonal change of flowering, fruiting and degree of depth make the views of the garden lively and versatile. For example, in the Autumn the bright red leaves of a maple tree *(Acer mono)* link well to the dark green leaves of Chinese junipers *(Juniperus chinensis)* and cypresses *(Taxodium ascendens, T. distichum)* or the orange-coloured fruits of the soap nut trees *(Sapindus mukorossi)* fully exposed after the leaves have fallen form an attractive contrast with broad-leaved trees which have retained their leaves.

In scenic spots, plants play the dominant role in composing landscapes. Natural assemblages of plants are retained and become the composition motif around which a garden is built.

In North China, such an approach is commonly used based on aged pine trees. These venerable giants have been carefully conserved and husbanded for hundreds of years. Even the emperors, when building their summer palaces, protected such stands by every means, simply because they are not only lively, unique specimens in the landscape but also out of respect for their great age and natural appearance.

The layout of plants in private Chinese gardens reached its zenith along the lower reaches of the Yangtse River. A wide variety of garden plants, including evergreen and deciduous trees and shrubs, her-

Courtyard of
a residence

baceous plants, vines and bamboos were used. In placing and integrating such a wide variety of plants the principles of contrast and harmony focusing on their figure, shape, colour and fragrance were used. The plantings were harmoniously coordinated with local conditions, architecture, rocks and waters to sketch out a unique and entrancing garden view.

TREATMENT OF HERBACEOUS SPECIES

In Chinese gardens, there are many ways of cultivating decorative herbaceous plants according to the size of the garden. In larger gardens, flowerbeds of either a single or several species are constructed. In the smaller, private classical gardens of Soochow, great ingenuity and resourcefulness resulted in many versatile and artistic styles for laying out decorative flower plants. In the front and at the back of halls, at the side of pavilions and galleries, by the pond side, and on the hill-foot, lake stone and yellow rocks are used to build up small flowerbeds to cultivate one or two herbaceous plants. Along pebble-paved pathways and around trees and sheds, tidy lily turf *(Liriope spicata)* and dwarf lily turf *(Ophiogogon japonica)* are planted. In the pond, aquatics such as lotus *(Nelumbo nucifera)* is planted in pots and sunk. Some water chestnuts *(Eleocharis tuberosa)* and cattails *(Acalypha hispida)* are planted along the water's edge to give a sense of wilderness.

THE ART OF MINIATURE LANDSCAPING IN POTS

Penjing (miniature trees and rockery) are commonly used as artistic focii in Chinese classical gardens. The history of Penjing can be traced back to the 7th century A.D. A fresco of "a maid holding a penjing in her hands" was found in the paved path leading to the tomb of Prince Zhang Huai of the Tang Dynasty in the 7th century.

Penjing is an ingenious art of complex beauty which employs artistic modelling of miniature landscapes in accordance with the qualities found in Nature. Artificially dwarfed plants of many species, unusual rocks and water are used to artistically imitate on a small scale the scenes of Nature. They are created in carefully selected vases, basins and pots. People praise them as "voiceless poems and stereoscopic pictures" — really, they are lively living pictures with seasonal changes and all the other qualities associated with moving landscapes.

Penjing are classified into two types according to source materials used: the "Shan Dan Penjing" (Rockery Penjing) and "Sudun Penjing" (Stump Penjing). A wide variety of styles have been developed over the centuries. The various landscapes found in Nature reappear in vivid and lively Penjing pots. They are the greatest achievements of artists and gardeners.

Penjing are used in the landscape out of door as a central focus in a small garden or in groups in a courtyard. They are used indoors to repeat or contrast with the landscape viewed from the building.

Qiang Hua Isle with the white pagoda in Bei Hai Park, Beijing.

9 *Practical Patterns of Chinese Gardens*

GARDENS IN BEIJING

Bei Hai

Bei Hai, now the North Sea Park, is located within the capital city and was established during the Jin Dynasty (1115 — 1234). The earliest palace garden in North China, it was originally a part of Xi Yuan (West Garden) which was one of the San Hai (Three Seas) to the west of the Imperial Palace, a long, narrow body of water between the garden and the Forbidden City.

The magnificent palace garden and the natural landscape of the three seas provide a striking contrast. The garden architecture and scenic spots were laid out along the waterside, so the field of vision is very wide. Qiong Hua Islet stands in the south-west portion of the lake. From the commanding elevation of the balcony around the white pagoda atop the islet the beholder surveys a panoramic view of the Imperial Palace, Jingshan Mountain and the scenes of the Mid-sea and South Sea. This islet is very large, so that some of the many buildings were constructed on its hill, while the pavilion, hall, kiosk and gallery are situated at the waterside. The latter are organized in three groups which were linked by a circular double-storey corridor which rises and falls with the topography of the islet. The architecture on the hillside includes rockeries, caves decorated with wonderful lake rocks, ornamental shrubs and herbaceous borders. The landscapes are spectacular and very natural.

The Summer Palace Garden

The Summer Palace Garden, the former Qing Yi Yuan (Clear Ripple Garden) located in the north-west suburb of Beijing was established during the reign of Emperor Qian Long in the middle of the 18th cen-

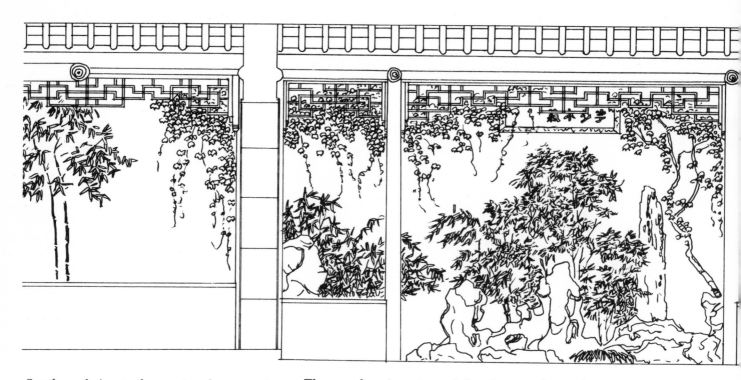

Southward view to the courtyard scene of Hua Bu Xiao Zhu (Small-size Ornamental construct).

tury. The garden is oriented in the north to the Longevity Hill Mo Shou Shan which stands about 60 meters high. The imperial court is symbolically situated to the east as is Kunming Lake in the west. This formal and symbolic layout of the palace is in marked contrast to the natural and bright character of the garden.

Kunming Lake occupies about 4/5 of the total area of Summer Palace Garden. On this broad water surface islets were built up, linked by bridges and long embankments that make waterscapes rich with architectural beauty, enriched and enlivened by diverse and remarkable planting of ornamental trees, shrubs and flowers. In front of the Longevity Hill, alongside the lake is a long gallery consisting of 273 rooms from which viewers can enjoy the diverse scenes created around the lake. The imperial palace, set on a hill facing the lake, is made up of a number of separate buildings. Pavilions, halls and courts extend down and around the slope to the foot of the hill where they join the Long Gallery.

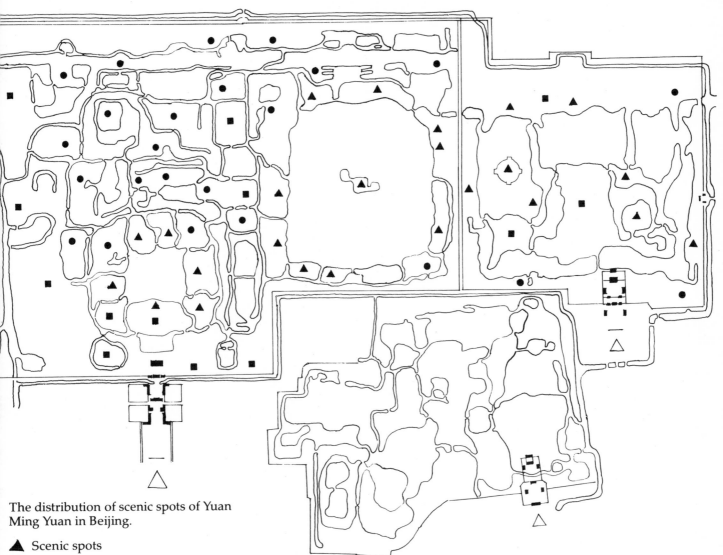

The distribution of scenic spots of Yuan Ming Yuan in Beijing.

▲ Scenic spots
● Small gardens
■ Architectural features

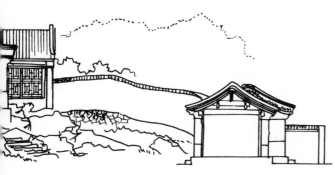

General elevation drawing of the Li Qing Xuan (Cleared-up-snowing Hall) architectural group in the Summer Palace of Beijing.

Practical Patterns of Chinese Gardens 153

The conception of the Summer Palace Garden is a complex integration of the magnificent imperial architecture typical of North China and the classical gardens developed in the Lower Reaches of the Yangtse River. Kunming Lake is a smaller but identical replication of the West Lake in Hangchow — even the separate scenes repeat those created in the South.

Bird's-eye view of Longevity Hall in the Summer Palace in Beijing.

The Yuan Ming Yuan Garden

Yuan Ming Yuan was undoubtedly the finest garden in North China before its destruction by British and French troops in 1860. Its priceless treasures — paintings, calligraphy, rare curios — were plundered. All the magnificent imperial buildings, together with wonderful aged trees and rare plants were burned to ashes. Only its ruins can be traced today.

This palace garden was conceived and largely constructed during the reign of Emperor Yong Zheng of the Qing Dynasty. From the early 18th century, for nearly 200 years through excellent management and ingenious administration, this unique imperial palace garden became world famous.

The total area of the garden was about 330 hectares (700 acres). It was made up of two parts: the Change Chun Yuan (Always Spring) Garden and Qi Chun (Gorgeous Spring) Yuan Garden, the latter attached to the former. In all, 40 separate scenic spots were created. The Yuan Ming Yuan Garden was built entirely on a flat site by sheer manpower piling up artificial hills from the excavation required for the lake. Seldom has so great and magnificent a garden been created.

Borassus flabellifer

Roystonea regia road

Placladus orientalis

Plate 11

Water scenery

Water scenery

Plate 12

As this palace garden was built on a large area it was conceived on a broad scale. Its buildings were varied in style and used to meet the ceremonial and administration requirements of the Imperial Family and its retinue and staff. The garden layout was organized in forty units which were designed as if independent but were ingeniously linked to each other to create an integrated network throughout the full extent of the garden. In keeping with the underlying topography created and the plants to be used, each of the 40 scenes forms a small garden consisting of a group of buildings, rockeries and ponds. Each was called "a garden within garden" or one of the "Forty Scenic Spots".

The Yuan Ming Yuan was conceived as a waterscape garden. The excavated lakes occupied more than half of the total area within the garden. The man-made hills and islets occupied another one-third of the total area of the garden. All the landscape scenes were organized around a watercourse, some larger and some smaller. All the watercourses were linked to each other in a perfectly integrated water system of lakes and ponds that blended harmoniously with the artificial man-made hills, rockeries, islets and embankments. The unifed waterscape and landscapes were artistic replications of well-known scenes in the region of the Lower Yangtse River.

The Yuan Ming Yuan bringing the Chang Chun Yuan and Qi Chun Yuan together in a single garden represented the most comprehensive and integrated classical garden of China.

At the northern side of the Chang Chun Yuan a set of European palaces in baroque and rococo styles was erected. They were designed and built under the supervision of F. Giuseppe Castiglione, an Italian missionary and painter then working in the Qing Court, and two Frenchmen, P. Michael Benoist and Jean Deni Attiret, during the reign of Emperor Qian Long (1736 — 1796).

The Palatial building Xie Qi Qu was constructed of marble, which was then carved. Columns were decorated with flower scrolls and

The ruins of a former European building at the site of the old Summer Palace (Yuan Ming Yuan).

The ruins of a former European building of Yuan Ming Yuan.

rows of leaves in Classical and Renaissance styles. Windows, balustrades and staircases were reminiscent of the luxurious furnishings associated with Versailles. The walls were decorated with multi-colored glazed bricks, and the roof topped with purple tiles. On each side of the main facade were two octagonal pavilions. A fountain was placed before the mansion. Trees and shrubs were planted and pruned in geometrical patterns in accordance with European fashion. Hedges, paths and sculptures imitated Western style.

At the present writing the Chinese government has inaugurated plans to rebuild the Yuan Ming Yuan Garden. Fortunately, the underlying topography of the man-made hills, lakes and the water system, though long since dried up still remains. The sites of the principle buildings can also be located. Moreover, a large number of blueprints, models and documents are available for reference. All of these elements will be of advantage in the restoration and reconstruction of this world-famous palace garden. It is to be deeply hoped that the original splendor of this remarkable garden can be recaptured in the near future.

Sectional and longitudinal section drawing of the middle architectural group in Zhou Zheng Yuan Garden of Soochow: A. Lu Yi Ting (Green Ripple Pavilion)   B. Xiang Xue Yun Wei Ting (Fragrant Snow and Colourful Cloud Pavilion)   C. Wu Zhu You Ji (Secluded Residence in Chinese Parasols and Bamboos)   D. Ji Hong Ting (Rainbow Pavilion for Rest)   E. Yuan Xiang Tang (Far-fragrant Pavilion)   F. Yao Men (Back Door).

A

B

C

D

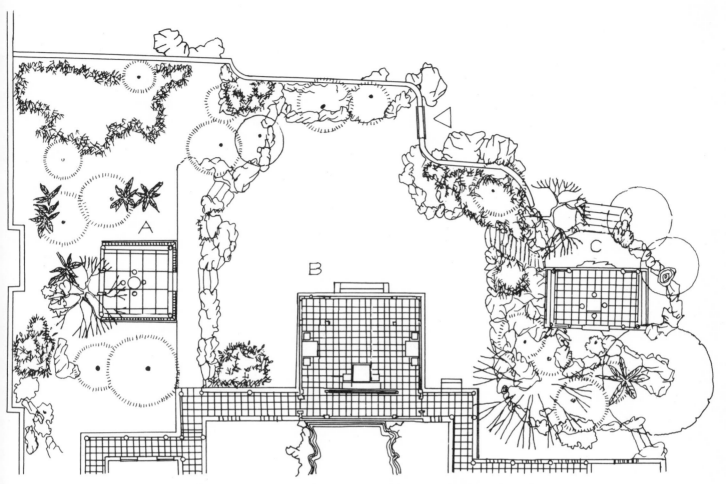

Plane figure of Pipa Yuan Garden (Loquat Garden) of Zhou Zheng Yuan Garden of Soochow.   A. Jia Shi Ting (Actually-good Pavilion)   B. Ling Long Guan (Exquisite Guesthouse)   C. Xiu Qi Ting (Beautifully-embroidered Pavilion).

Practical Patterns of Chinese Gardens 157

The Zhou Zheng Yuan Garden

The Zhou Zheng Yuan Garden is located in the north-east precincts of the city of Soochow. It is one of the four famous classical gardens in the region of the lower reaches of Yangtse River. This garden was established during the reign of Emperor Jia Jing of the Ming Dynasty in the middle of the 16th century.

Originally, the center of the Zhou Zheng Yuan Garden was a water-logged depression. The garden designer took the advantage of this natural site by deepening it into a pond and using it as the key element in creating a waterscape garden. In this way he achieved twice the result with half the effort.

Entering the eastern entrance gate to the garden, the first sight greeting a visitor is a rockery which blocks any further view of the garden. The viewer passes through a cave in the rockery which leads to a gallery at the back of the rockery standing before a pond. From this gallery the beautiful scenes of the garden suddenly appear before the viewer.

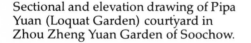

Sectional and elevation drawing of Pipa Yuan (Loquat Garden) courtyard in Zhou Zheng Yuan Garden of Soochow.

The general layout was based on water scenes with the building mainly on the south and east sides of the garden. Trees and decorative shrubs occupy most of the north side. The watercourse was divided into several separate lakes and ponds of different sizes and shapes by embankments. Bridges linked various parts of the garden to form a perfect waterscape.

The rockeries erected in the watercourses harmonize or contrast with the trees, rocks and pavilions situated along and around the waterscenes. The rise and fall of the bridges and embankment create a strong contrast with the architectural group to the south. On the north side of the lake, a pavilion and kiosk were built at the foot of the hill near the water. The watercourse here is long and narrow extending in zigzag fashion to the southwest. Corridors were built on both sides of the pond to form a water courtyard. The structures of the garden are mainly pavilions, halls, and corridors, named according to the various scenes.

The pleasure boat pavilion at Xiang Zhou (Fragrant Islet) in Zhou Zheng Yuan Garden.

The water kiosk, Xiao Cang Lang (Small Blue Wave), of Zhou Zheng Yuan Garden of Soochow.

Sectional and longitudinal section drawing, viewing northwards to the courtyard of Pipa Yuan Garden (Loquat Garden) of Hu Yuan Garden in Soochow.

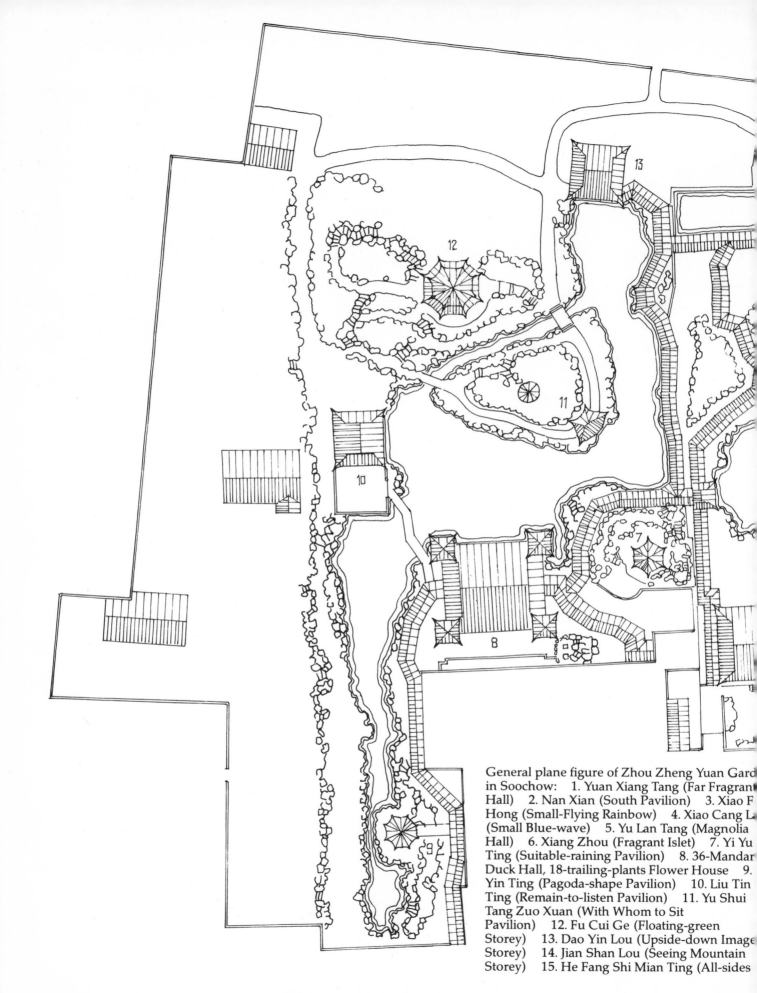

General plane figure of Zhou Zheng Yuan Garden in Soochow: 1. Yuan Xiang Tang (Far Fragrant Hall) 2. Nan Xian (South Pavilion) 3. Xiao Fei Hong (Small-Flying Rainbow) 4. Xiao Cang Lang (Small Blue-wave) 5. Yu Lan Tang (Magnolia Hall) 6. Xiang Zhou (Fragrant Islet) 7. Yi Yu Ting (Suitable-raining Pavilion) 8. 36-Mandarin Duck Hall, 18-trailing-plants Flower House 9. Yin Ting (Pagoda-shape Pavilion) 10. Liu Tin Ting (Remain-to-listen Pavilion) 11. Yu Shui Tang Zuo Xuan (With Whom to Sit Pavilion) 12. Fu Cui Ge (Floating-green Storey) 13. Dao Yin Lou (Upside-down Image Storey) 14. Jian Shan Lou (Seeing Mountain Storey) 15. He Fang Shi Mian Ting (All-sides

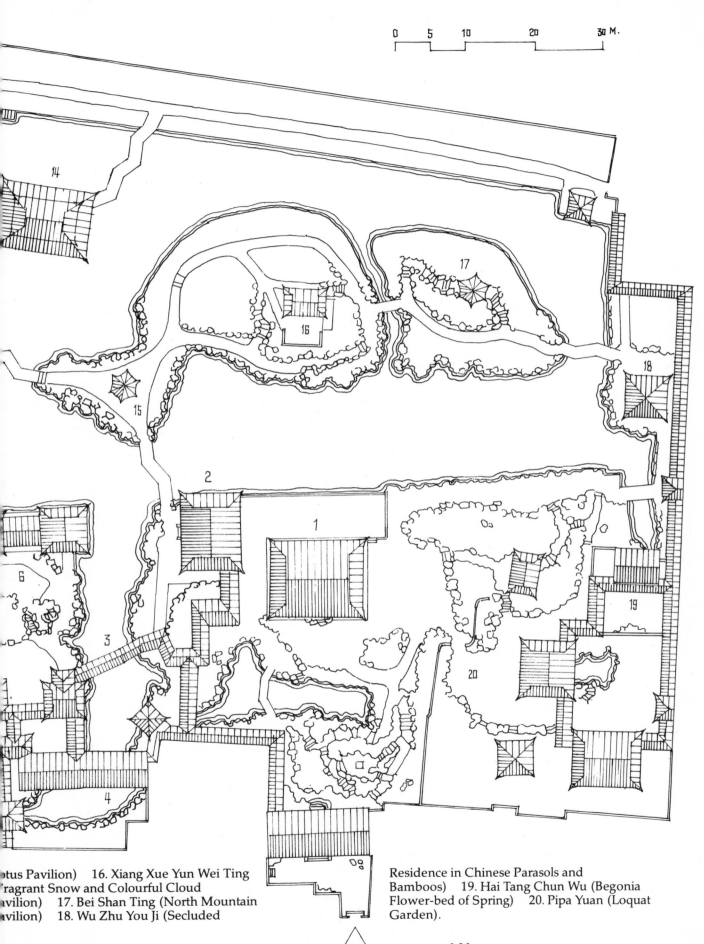

otus Pavilion)　16. Xiang Xue Yun Wei Ting
ragrant Snow and Colourful Cloud
avilion)　17. Bei Shan Ting (North Mountain
avilion)　18. Wu Zhu You Ji (Secluded

Residence in Chinese Parasols and
Bamboos)　19. Hai Tang Chun Wu (Begonia
Flower-bed of Spring)　20. Pipa Yuan (Loquat
Garden).

161

The Liu Yuan Garden

The Liu Yuan Garden outside Soochow was established during the reign of Emperor Dao Guang of the Qing Dynasty at the beginning of the 19th century. It was originally a private residence garden of the Liu family and acquired by the Emperor. The garden was divided into three parts: the large rockeries in the west, forested with Chinese sweet gum trees, decorated with pavilions and surrounded by water; the middle part consisted of a number of ponds, embellished with pavilions and rocks and linked to each other by long corridors and small bridges; and the east part, originally the Liu's residence of big halls, small rooms, a veranda with windows and buildings separated by whitewashed cloud (high) walls.

The small-size courtyard of Yi Feng Xuan (Bowing-peak Veranda with windows) of Liu Yuan Garden in Soochow.

The spacious front hall was connected to the garden entrance by an elaborate gate structure. From there the viewer walked along a somewhat narrow passageway, which turned twice, leading him to an open hall facing a courtyard named Gu Mu Jiao Ke (Crisscross-branch Aged Tree), the first scenic spot of the garden proper. The narrow passageway was partly in the shade and partly in the open. Small scenes planted with shade or sun-loving plants were planted outside with apertures in the sidewalls. So a rich and varied array of scenes met the visitors on their way to Gu Mu Jiao Ke which was originally the southern high, whitewashed, enclosing wall of the Liu's residence. The ingenious garden designer reserved an aged, huge, magnificent tree there. Four large Chinese characters "Gu Mu Jiao Ke" of splendid calligraphy were carved in the wall. Under the carving a beautiful flower bed was built against the wall. This scene, though very simple and in a limited space, is very attractive and picturesque. The whitewashed wall as a background looks like drawing paper and provides a background reminiscent of that in ink paintings.

Plane figure of Crisscross Aged-trees and Hua Bu Xiao Zhu (Small-size Ornamental Construct) in the Liu Yuan Garden of Soochow:
A. Crisscross Aged-trees
B. Hua Bu Xiao Zhu
C. Lu Yin (Green Shade).

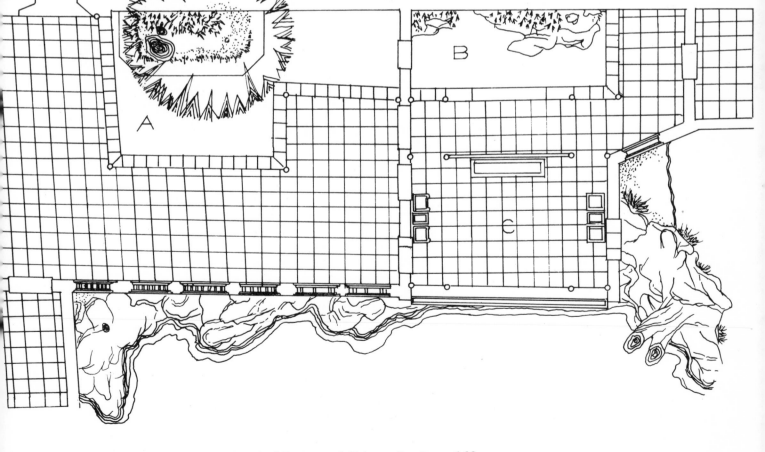

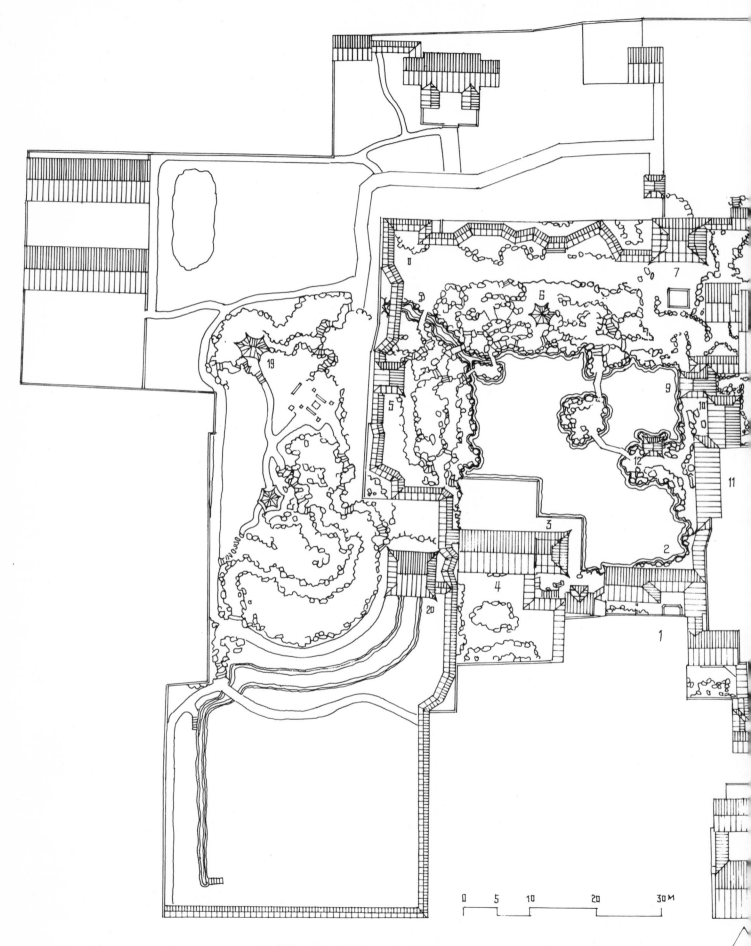

164 *The Garden Art of China*

General plane figure of Liu Yuan Garden in Soochow:
1. Gu Mu Jiao Ke (Crisscross-branch Aged Trees)
2. Lu Yin (Green Shade)
3. Min Se Lou (Bright Twenty Five String Instrument Hall)
4. Han Bi Shan Fang (Conserve Green Mountain House)
5. Wen Mu Xi Xian Xuan (Smelling Osmanthus Fragrance Pavilion)
6. Ke Ting (Ke Pavilion)
7. Yan Cui Ge (Far Green Two-storeyed Pavilion)
8. Wu Fang Xian Guan (Five-peak Fairy Hall)
9. Quin Feng Chi Guan (Breezy Pond Pavilion)
10. Xi Lou (West Storey)
11. Qu Xi Lou (Bend Creek Pavilion)
12. Hou Pu Pavilion
13. Huan Wo Du Shu Chu (Returning to My Reading Room)
14. Yi Feng Xuan (Bowing-peak Pavilion)
15. Yuan Yang Ting (Mandarin Duck Hall)
16. Guan Yun Lou (Cloud-crowned Storey).

From two octagonal openings in the wall to the west, a rockery, a pond and courtyard appear indistinctly in the back of Lu Yin (Green Shade). While through a small door the viewer sees a smaller courtyard decorated only with a few wonderful rocks and some scattered green bamboos — very simple but quiet and tasteful. On a carved wooden floral screen standing at the back of the courtyard, the beholders can see depicted all the garden views. This screen is a prelude to point out the motifs of the garden.

After viewing the rockery and water courtyard, the visitor comes to a richly decorated parlour in which to rest before continuing his tour. This parlour is connected to a gallery of several sections each in a different style. This gallery is quite extraordinary for in a compactly organized space a complex but harmonious gallery system gives the viewer a marked sense of change of space.

Along through the gallery passage to Qu Xi Lou (Bend Creek Pavilion), apertures were placed in the walls for viewing the outside scenes. Then the visitor turns to the right to Xi Lou (West Storey) in an inner courtyard which is three steps higher than Qu Xi Lou. This change of level provides a clear contrast between the two scenes. The visitor next comes to Qing Feng Chi Guan (Breezy Pond Pavilion) which is a water kiosk open to the west for viewing the scenic rockery and pond from a different prospective.

Onward to the east, the first scene to appear is Wu Fang Xian Guan (Five Peak Fairy Hall) made of namu. (*Phoebe namu*, Lauraceae, an exquisite timber produced in Yunnan, Szechwan, Kweichow, Kwangsi

Min Se Lou Hall of Liu Yuan Garden, Soochow.

and Hunan Provinces. There are seven species in the genus. The tree reaches 30 m high with a 1.5 m diameter and is very straight, so its timber was used to build palaces and royal gardens. As the timber is fragrant and durable, it was used traditionally to make coffins for kings, emperors, royal family members and high officials.) It is separated into two parts by a concave/convex wooden screen to give a sense of deepening in space. To the north, three peaks made of lake rocks, named Guan Yun (Crown Cloud), Dua Yun (Floral Cloud), Xiu Yun (Hilly Cloud), were laid out. Beside this scene is a five-room pavilion, Guan Yun Lou (Cloud-crowned Storey), for viewing the

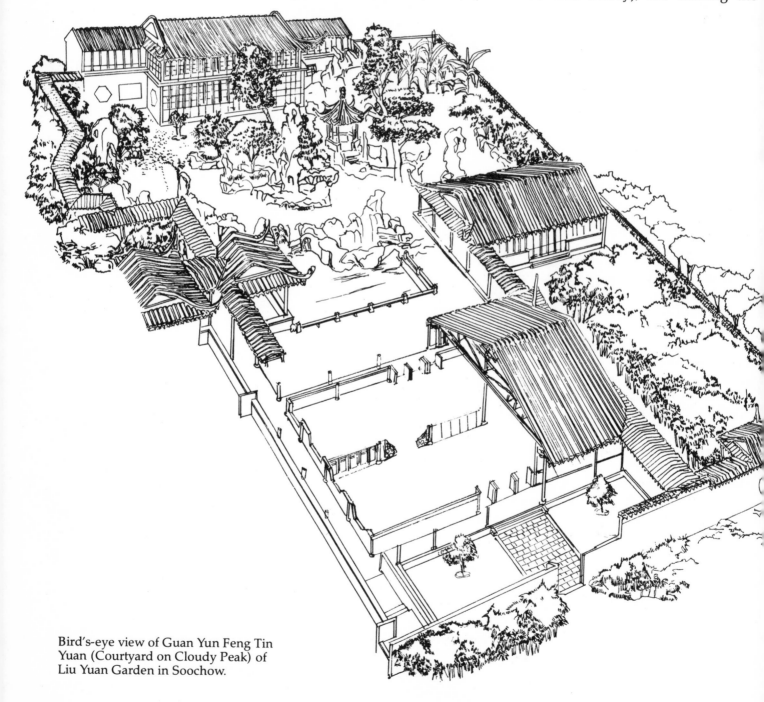

Bird's-eye view of Guan Yun Feng Tin Yuan (Courtyard on Cloudy Peak) of Liu Yuan Garden in Soochow.

scenery on Hu Qiu Shan (Tiger Hill) far away. This setting makes a nice contrast with the rockeries in the middle ground and the architectural group of pavilions and halls at the east end of the garden.

From Wu Fang Xian Guan going along a short, shaded, zigzag corridor, embellished with vines and flowers, the visitor comes to a two-and-a-half room study. Its windows facing south are embellished with floral designs on dark redwood frames in harmonious contrast to the surrounding white wall. The half room was created by a fan-shaped screen that strengthens the quiet atmosphere. Through the windows, the viewer sees bamboos and wonderful rocks and flowers like variant pieces of vivid paintings. A small courtyard planted with bamboos

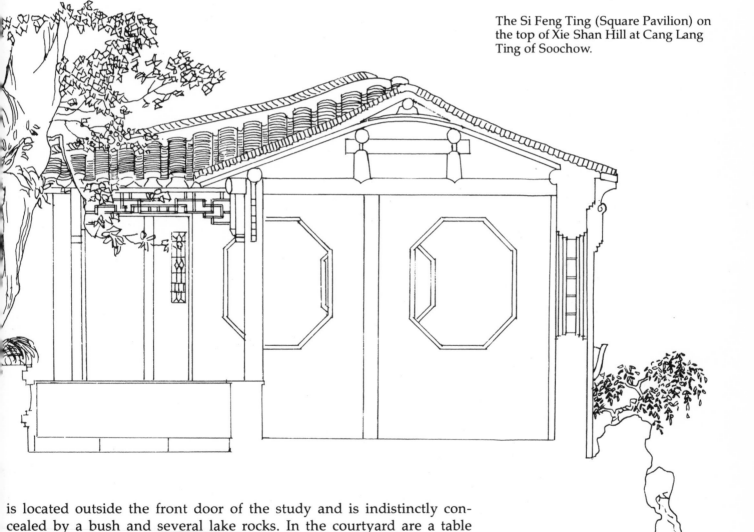

The Si Feng Ting (Square Pavilion) on the top of Xie Shan Hill at Cang Lang Ting of Soochow.

is located outside the front door of the study and is indistinctly concealed by a bush and several lake rocks. In the courtyard are a table and some drum-shaped stools at which the visitors may rest.

Finally, going westward along a broad corridor to a creek where a water kiosk stands over the water, the visitor returns to the Front Hall.

The features of this garden represent the best of private residence gardening in Soochow.

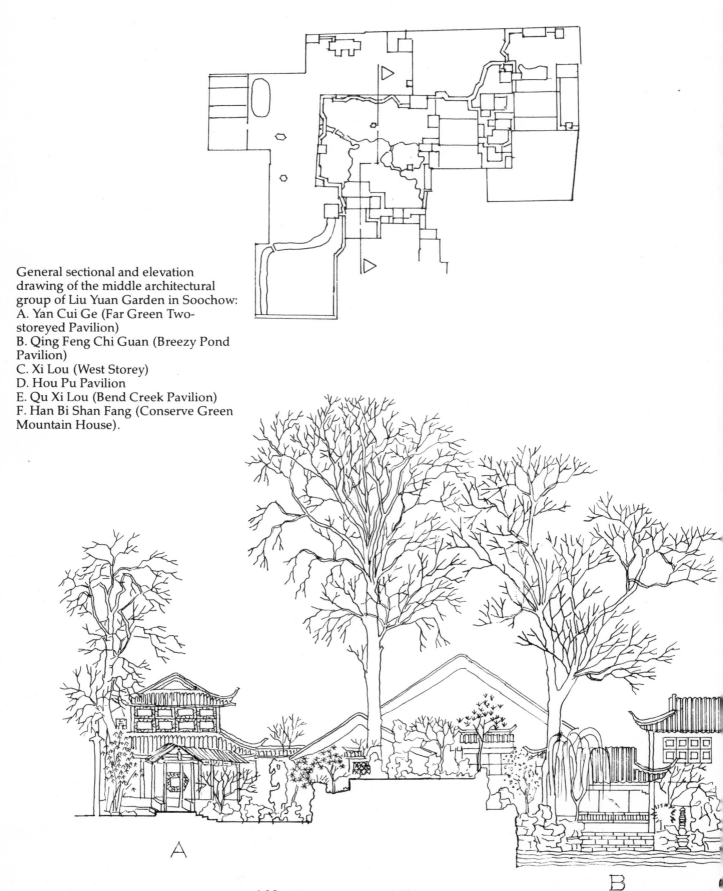

General sectional and elevation drawing of the middle architectural group of Liu Yuan Garden in Soochow:
A. Yan Cui Ge (Far Green Two-storeyed Pavilion)
B. Qing Feng Chi Guan (Breezy Pond Pavilion)
C. Xi Lou (West Storey)
D. Hou Pu Pavilion
E. Qu Xi Lou (Bend Creek Pavilion)
F. Han Bi Shan Fang (Conserve Green Mountain House).

A

B

Sectional drawing of Lu Yin (Green Shade) and
viewing eastward to the courtyard scene of Hua Bu
Xiao Zhu (Small House for Walking-around).

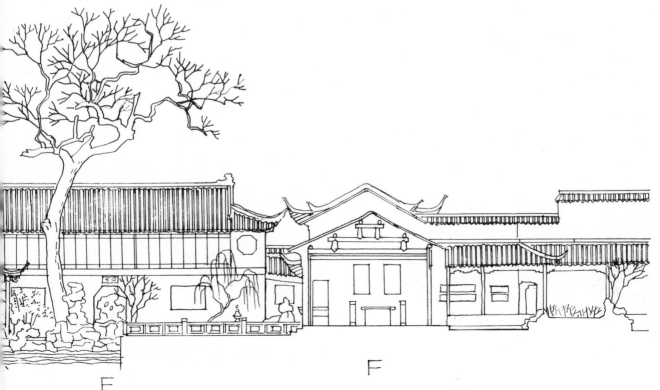

E

F

Practical Patterns of Chinese Gardens **169**

Garden scene of Yi Yuan Garden, Soochow

In Shi Zi Lin Garden (Lion Grove), Soochow.

In Shi Zi Lin (Lion Grove), Soochow.

Early spring scene in Zhou Zheng Yuan Garden, Soochow.

Veranda with windows alongside a small goldfish pond in Wang Si Yuan Garden in Soochow.

Chinese flowering crabapples in Zhou Zheng Yuan Garden.

Bird's-eye view of the middle part of Wang Shi Yuan Garden in Soo

The Wang Shi Yuan Garden

Wang Shi Yuan Garden is located in the south-east section of the city of Soochow. It was built during the Southern Song Dynasty at the beginning of the 12th century. Though not large, the delicately wrought garden design assures its fame among the classical gardens of Soochow.

Wang Shi Yuan was a private residence garden compactly laid out in a limited space with variant scenes. The residential compound consisted of three rows of spacious houses along a south to north axis. The front hall, main hall, and back hall, were delicately embellished with well-crafted furniture, splendid calligraphy and painting. Passageways were constructed from the halls to reach both the rockery, where a remarkable study was situated at the top, and to the main garden and the inner garden.

Though the water surface of the pond is not large, structures were built around the water side in cleverly understated fashion. The embankments were protected by a revetment made of antique yellow stones, to make the lake look more extensive. The pond was nearly square with revetments of concave and convex style, as in lava flows, that result in a splendid artistic effect. At the corners in the north-west and south-east, twisting creeks were excavated to provide water. The Zhou Ying Shui Ge (Tassel-wash Water Pavilion) was positioned in a relatively low site while at the west side a corridor climbed upward to the Yu Dao Fang Lai Ting (Moon-wind-coming Pavilion). From Yu Dao Fang Lai Ting the visitor has a commanding view to overlook all the scenes in the garden. At the north end of the corridor a zigzag bridge placed close to the water surface markedly widens the visual perception of the lake. Along the sides of the creek entering the lake at this point, bushes were planted to provide a sense of wilderness. A three-bend small bridge and an arch bridge were built at proportionable heights over the creek both for traffic and as embellishments adding much charm to the scene.

Sectional and longitudinal section drawing of Osmanthus Pavilion facing north to small hilly land in Wang Shi Yuan Garden of Soochow.

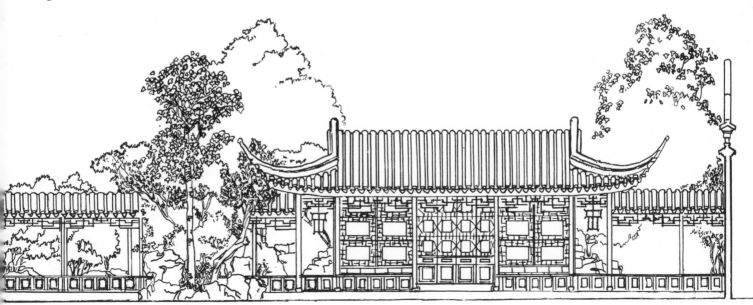

From the Yu Dao Fang Lai Ting the viewer travels along a corridor northward to Kan Song Du Hua Xian (See Pines and Paintings Hall), to the rockeries and flower beds laid out beside the creek. Then turning back through the tortuous corridor at the back of Zhou Ying Shui Ge he passes through the Xiao Shan Cong Gui Xuan (Small Hilly Grove Osmanthus Pavilion), which is a roundabout path past the residence house to a water kiosk which is one of the primary scenic spots. This kiosk was paired with another on the opposite side of the lake. The viewer can see from either the scenes around the lakeside. The careful layout and creative use of the waterscenes leads the viewer of this small garden to feel that it is visually larger.

From the Kan Song Du Hua Xian looking southward is the picturesque flower bed dominated by pines and cypresses on the north side. These tangible outside scenes are balanced and blended with the brush paintings mounted in the hall, greatly enriching the esthetic splendour of the scene.

In the western part is the Dian Chun Yi Garden — an inner garden (Ming Xuan is the replica of this garden). Its name came from a verse "The peony flowers richly even at the end of Spring" of a Chinese poem describing the beautiful peony growing in a spare planting before a flower bed in front of the hall. In the front courtyard of the hall a rockery was placed opposite a zigzag corridor at the southwest corner. A fountain named Han Bi (Source of Clear Water), provides a continuous flow of fresh water to a pond in the middle part of the garden. Above this fountain a half-pavilion named Leng Quan (Cold Fountain), was erected. Rock cliffs were built on the south side.

The environment created in this small inner garden gives a great sense of seclusion. It is small wonder that this garden furnished the model for the Ming Xuan Gardens in Yangchow.

Yangchow is one of the old cities famous for its culture and beautiful landscapes. It is situated on the lower reaches of Yangtse River. Shou Xi Hu (Thin West Lake) is one of the best known scenic areas in China. The city extended eastward from this splendid natural feature. Undoubtedly Yangchow's fine gardens were inspired by it. It is still located in the west suburb of the city. The Chinese word Shou (thin) means delicate and pretty, to describe the beauty of the lake.

Sectional and elevation drawing of the middle architectural group in Wang Shi Yuan Garden of Soochow.

Wang Shi Yuan Garden in Soochow.

Practical Patterns of Chinese Gardens 175

Shou Xi Hu was originally a braided network of rivers. Years of dredging and merging ultimately resulted in the composition of an irregular rectangular lake, whose water surface was dotted with islets. Along the lakeside, weeping willows *(Salix babylonica)* were planted in rows waving their numerous soft branches to and fro in a gentle breeze. On the wider part of the lake, the scenic Wu Ting Qiao (Five Pavilion Bridge), Bai Ta Xin Yun (White Pagoda and Blue Sky) and Xiao Jing Shan (Small Golden Hill) were built and are outstandingly beautiful sights to behold.

As there were no high mountains in the surroundings, the private residence gardens were built along or close to the lake. The styles used in building pavilions, bridges, halls and galleries were greatly varied and exquisitely designed. Every rock or tree was selected with equal care to harmonize with the structures and compensate for the absence of hills and mountains. The lake provided the water route to visit the numerous scenic spots and gardens. The irregular rectangular water surface was divided by embankments and bridges, to provide a feeling of variety and difference.

The well-known scenic spots of Shou Xi Hu are:

Si Quiao Yi Yu (Four Bridges in Misty Rain) is one of the finest scenic spots on Shou Xi Hu. This scene was created by three small islets in a bay of the lake. The four bridges linked the islets to the lake's embankment and to each other so that sightseers could enjoy the entire scene. The hazy picture created on misty rainy days is splendid and attracts much interest.

Xiao Jing Shan (Small Golden Hill) was a small hill artificially piled up in the central part of the lake similar to the shape of Jing Shan in Zhen Jiang on the southern bank of the Yangtse River. This was the center of a waterscape. A group of structures built on the hill were placed so the viewers can see the scenes around the lakeside.

Sectional and elevation drawing of Osmanthus Hall courtyard among a small group of rockeries in Wang Shi Yuan Garden of Soochow.

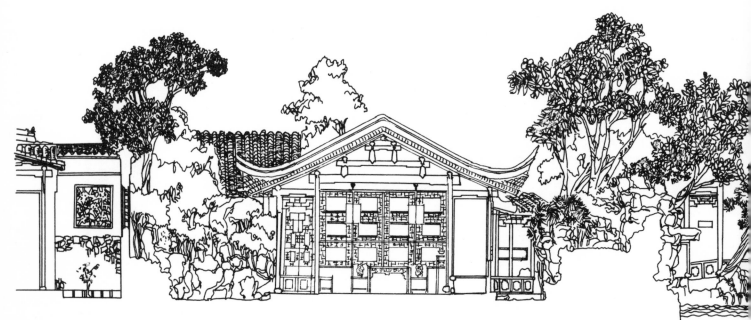

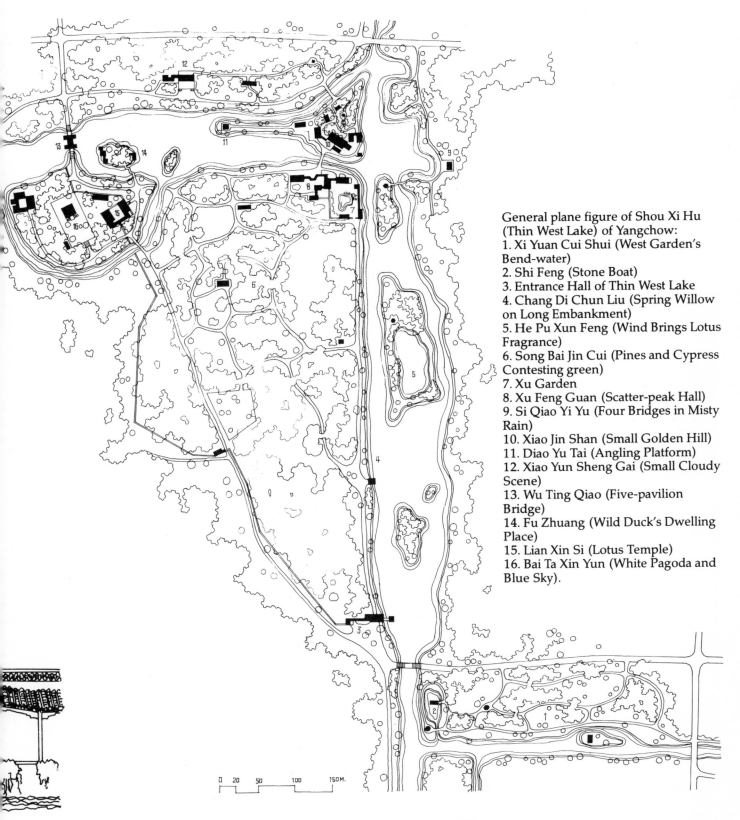

General plane figure of Shou Xi Hu (Thin West Lake) of Yangchow:
1. Xi Yuan Cui Shui (West Garden's Bend-water)
2. Shi Feng (Stone Boat)
3. Entrance Hall of Thin West Lake
4. Chang Di Chun Liu (Spring Willow on Long Embankment)
5. He Pu Xun Feng (Wind Brings Lotus Fragrance)
6. Song Bai Jin Cui (Pines and Cypress Contesting green)
7. Xu Garden
8. Xu Feng Guan (Scatter-peak Hall)
9. Si Qiao Yi Yu (Four Bridges in Misty Rain)
10. Xiao Jin Shan (Small Golden Hill)
11. Diao Yu Tai (Angling Platform)
12. Xiao Yun Sheng Gai (Small Cloudy Scene)
13. Wu Ting Qiao (Five-pavilion Bridge)
14. Fu Zhuang (Wild Duck's Dwelling Place)
15. Lian Xin Si (Lotus Temple)
16. Bai Ta Xin Yun (White Pagoda and Blue Sky).

Practical Patterns of Chinese Gardens   177

Diao Yu Tai (Angle Platform) was placed at the side of the lake opposite Wu Ting Qiao and Bai Ta Xin Yun (White Pagoda and Blue Sky). It was built during the reign of Emperor Qian Long of the Qing Dynasty in the middle of the 18th century. It is said that he had angled here during his tour of inspection of Yangchow. The walls of the platform along the waterside were pierced by two doors, one facing the Wu Ting Qiao and the other focusing on the White Pagoda. The purpose of these doors was of Jie Jing (to borrow scenes).

Fu Zhuang (Wild Duck's Dwelling Place) was a miniature group of structures built in the lake. They looked like wild ducks floating on the water, hence the name. They were placed to embellish the scene presented by the lake.

Wu Ting Qiao (Five Pavilion Bridge) is well-known for its beautiful modelling. There are five pavilions on the bridge, the center one being the highest while the remaining four were symmetrically balanced in height and size. There were fifteen bridge openings and four wings underneath. Its unique scene was carefully planned so as to reflect the moon in every bridge opening during moonlit nights.

Shou Xi Hu (Thin West Lake).

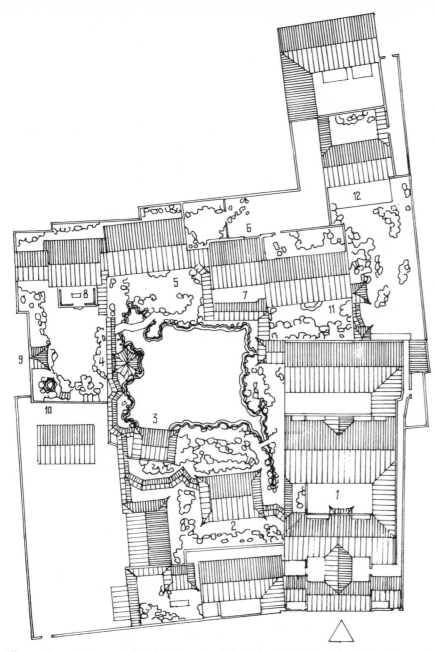

General plane figure of Wang Shi Yuan Garden in Soochow:
1. Residence
2. Xiao Shan Cong Gui Xuan (Small Hilly Grove Osmanthus Pavilion)
3. Zhou Ying Shui Ge (Tassel-wash Water Pavilion)
4. Yu Dao Fang Lai Ting (Moon-wind-coming Pavilion)
5. Kan Song Du Hua Xian (See Pines and Paintings Hall)
6. Ji Xu Zhai (Abstract-collection Study Room)
7. Zhu Wai Yi Zhi Xian (Branch Pavilion Outside Bamboos)
8. Dian Chun Yi Garden (Ming Xuan is the replica of this garden)
9. Leng Quan Ting (Cool-well Pavilion)
10. Han Bi Xian (Conserve Green Well)
11. Wu Fang Shu Wu (Five-peak Study Room)
12. Ti Yun Lou (Stair-room).

Ping Shan Tang (Flat Mountain Hall) located on the Shu Gang Hillock in the north-west suburb of Yangchow is the commanding ground within the area of the lake. From the front of this hall, viewers see the mountains across the Yangtse River to the south as if they were on the same level, so it was named Ping Shan (Flat Mountains).

The famous Chinese writers Ouyang Xiu and Su Dong Pu of the Southern Song Dynasty in the 11th century lived here for a time. An old temple Da Ming Si established in the 5th century still stood at that time. In the middle of the 8th century, a famous monk Jian Zhen of this temple went to Japan on six separate occasions to help Japanese Buddhists establish that religion in the island kingdom. A memorial hall in Japanese style was subsequently erected on Shu Gang Hillock in his honour.

On the west side of Ping Shan Hall is an ancient garden called the West Garden. The unique features of this Chinese classical garden are its huge, aged trees and wonderful rocks.

Ge Guan Garden in Yangchow city was established early in the 19th century. The garden is famous for its numerous bamboos. Its name derives from the similarity to the Chinese character for the leaves of bamboo. The Chinese character for Ge is similar to the appearance of the bamboo leaves. This was a private residence garden famous for its rockeries of yellow stones called Si Ji Shan Se (Mountain Colours of Four Seasons).

Through the entrance lane beside the residence house stood a solitary, aged *Wisteria sinensis,* hundreds of years old. Further along are two flower beds flanking the lane and bordered along the bank of the beds by slender bamboos intermittantly mingled with stalagmites to symbolize a mountain forest in Spring time. Behind the bamboos is a floral wall with a full moon-shaped door. This is the garden gate proper. Above it, on a horizontal slab are inscribed the two Chinese characters Ge Yuan in splendid calligraphy.

The scenic spots of Shou Xi Hu in Yangchow.

On passing through the moongate the first sight is Quihua Ting (Osmanthus Hall) with osmanthus trees in the front and a pond at the back. Along the border wall on the north side, a seven-storey gallery connected by corridors provides access to the rockeries. From the highest level of the gallery viewers can see all the scenes of the garden. Because the way to the rockery was planted to provide a sense of Spring, the rockery was named Chun Shan (Spring Rockery).

Along the north pond side, a pair of boat-shaped pavilions, the Yuan Yang Ting (Mandarin Duck Pavilion) were placed to face a hexagonal pavilion on the opposite bank. On the west side of the pond, a rockery was built up of lake stones and planted with pines and other trees. From a cave at the base of the rockery flows a stream to feed the lake. The stream is crossed by a zigzag bridge close to the rockery and overhung by marvellously shaped green-gray lake stones projecting from the built-up mountain. The environment created by this ingenious rockery is comfortable and cool. It is called Xia Shan (Summer Rockery).

To the south of this rockery a bamboo forest was planted on a built-up hill. The forest is reached by walking up steps made of lake stone. The path through the forest returns the viewer to the seven storey corridor by way of Xue Pu (The Library of Classics) — a restful place for study. A corridor leads the viewer on to the large yellow stone piled-up rockery on the east side, at the top of which is a pavilion. A set of steps winds up this rockery on the west side. Half way up these steps the viewer coming at nightfall sees the reddish sunset reflected on the yellow stones. It is like a colorful picture of autumn leaves — red and yellow. So it was named Qiu Shan (Autumn Rockery).

Taking advantage of a different position, direction and materials used, a fourth rockery was built. The Dong Shan (Winter Rockery) was made of yellow-brown stones which contrast harmoniously with the dark green pines and cypresses planted nearby. A large cavern was built into the rockery. From its ceiling the wonderful sight of stalactites can be indistinctly seen in the dim light provided by a strategically placed crevice. Further inside the cavern were built a small courtyard, bridge and a room — all made of yellow stones. From here the viewer follows the steps winding out to a pavilion high on the rockery. From this commanding ground he can see the peaks of all rockeries below him as well as all the scenes of Shou Xi Hu (Thin West Lake). There is a gallery on the south side also giving access to the rockery. Beside its foot stands a hall and a white rockery of piled-up stones from Xuancheng and Anhui provinces positioned against a white-washed wall facing north. This rockery symbolizes a snow-covered hill in wintertime.

Ge Yuan was inspired by the theme used repeatedly in traditional Chinese painting, of the mountains or hills used in the Springtime for touring, in the Summer for sightseeing, in the Autumn for climbing and in the Winter for living in safety and serenity.

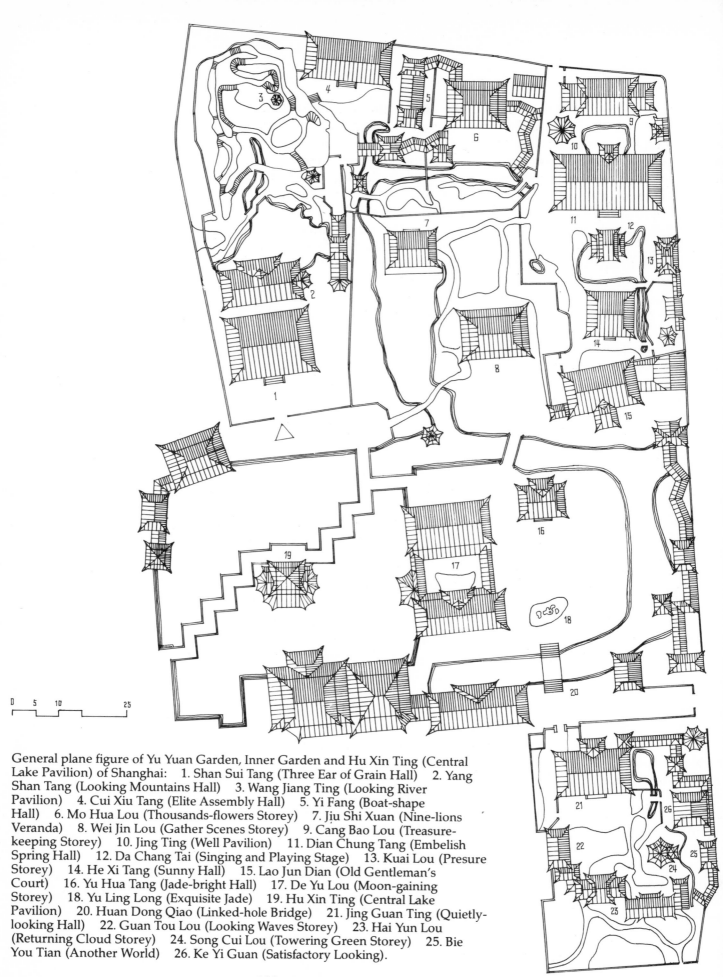

General plane figure of Yu Yuan Garden, Inner Garden and Hu Xin Ting (Central Lake Pavilion) of Shanghai: 1. Shan Sui Tang (Three Ear of Grain Hall)   2. Yang Shan Tang (Looking Mountains Hall)   3. Wang Jiang Ting (Looking River Pavilion)   4. Cui Xiu Tang (Elite Assembly Hall)   5. Yi Fang (Boat-shape Hall)   6. Mo Hua Lou (Thousands-flowers Storey)   7. Jiu Shi Xuan (Nine-lions Veranda)   8. Wei Jin Lou (Gather Scenes Storey)   9. Cang Bao Lou (Treasure-keeping Storey)   10. Jing Ting (Well Pavilion)   11. Dian Chung Tang (Embelish Spring Hall)   12. Da Chang Tai (Singing and Playing Stage)   13. Kuai Lou (Presure Storey)   14. He Xi Tang (Sunny Hall)   15. Lao Jun Dian (Old Gentleman's Court)   16. Yu Hua Tang (Jade-bright Hall)   17. De Yu Lou (Moon-gaining Storey)   18. Yu Ling Long (Exquisite Jade)   19. Hu Xin Ting (Central Lake Pavilion)   20. Huan Dong Qiao (Linked-hole Bridge)   21. Jing Guan Ting (Quietly-looking Hall)   22. Guan Tou Lou (Looking Waves Storey)   23. Hai Yun Lou (Returning Cloud Storey)   24. Song Cui Lou (Towering Green Storey)   25. Bie You Tian (Another World)   26. Ke Yi Guan (Satisfactory Looking).

The scenic areas of this garden were separated by high walls. Access to each area is by doorways and other apertures of different shapes in the wall. These openings were conceived in terms of picture frames to frame the different and distinct scenes in each area. Ge Yuan Garden is one of the most unique and carefully designed examples of landscape gardening in China.

A pair of bronze lions in Yu Yuan Garden of Shanghai

Yu Yuan Garden (Comfort Garden) is located on the north side of the Chenghuang Miao (The Town's God Temple) in old Shanghai City. This garden was established during the reign of Emperor Jia Jing of the Ming Dynasty in the middle of the 16th century. Yu Yuan Garden is the oldest classical garden in Shanghai with a history of four hundred and more years. Originally a private garden built by Pan Yungrui in the Ming Dynasty for his aged father, Pan En, the Minister of Punishments in feudal China, to enjoy in his retirement. Ownership of this private garden changed several times. It is now being renewed and managed by Shanghai Municipal Administration. As it was sited in the west, it had another name Xi Yuan (West Garden) while its companion garden Nei Yuan to the east is sometimes called Nei Yuan (East Garden). Inside the garden gate, two halls were set on opposite sides of the garden path San Sui Tang (Three Ears of Grain Hall) and Yang Shan Tang (Hall for Looking Upward). Both are 2-storied structures built to frame the view of the nearby pond with a water kiosk.

In the north-west corner stands a large rockery made of yellow stones on an earthen foundation. A fountain in the form of a spring was placed in the rockery. The water flowed in a zigzag course down to a small valley which supplied the pond. From the top deck of a two-storey bridge built in front of the rockery viewers overlook the scenes inside the garden as well as along the Huangpu River outside the garden. From the lawn viewers entered a pavilion placed under the deep shade of Chinese parasol trees (*Firmiana simplex*) for visitors to rest. At the foot of the rockery, the creek flowed parallel with a floral wall pierced by ringlike apertures just above the water. Scenes outside the garden are reflected in the clear water.

On the east side of Chenghuang Miao is the Nei Yuan Garden (East Garden) which was established during the reign of Emperor Kang Xi of the Qing Dynasty at the beginning of the 18th century. Although this garden was not large, its design was quite unique and exquisite. The Tsui Hsiu Tang (Hall of Elegance), the main structure in the garden, faced a rockery. On the top of the rockery a small pavilion was built which reflects the image of the pavilion in the clear water of a pond placed beneath it. The water for this pond flowed from a stone dragon's mouth. Visitors then followed a zigzag corridor to come back to Tsui Hsiu Tang to view the scenes alongside the Huangpu River of Shanghai.

Entrance of Nei Yuan (East Garden) of Yu Yuan Garden.

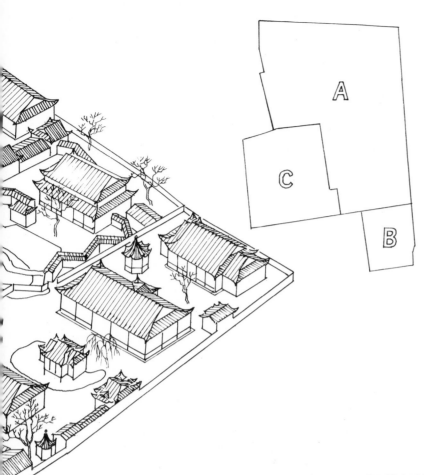

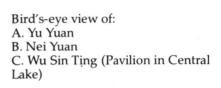

Bird's-eye view of:
A. Yu Yuan
B. Nei Yuan
C. Wu Sin Ting (Pavilion in Central Lake)

Yangshan Tang (Hall) in Yu Yuan Garden of Shanghai.

Practical Patterns of Chinese Gardens 185

THE GARDENS IN WUSIH

Ji Chang Yuan Garden of Wusih is one of the most famous gardens in the region of the lower reaches of the Yangtse River. It is located at the eastern foot of Wei Shan Mountain, and was built during the reign of Emperor Zheng De of the Ming Dynasty at the beginning of the 16th century.

The Ji Chang Yuan Garden of Wusih.

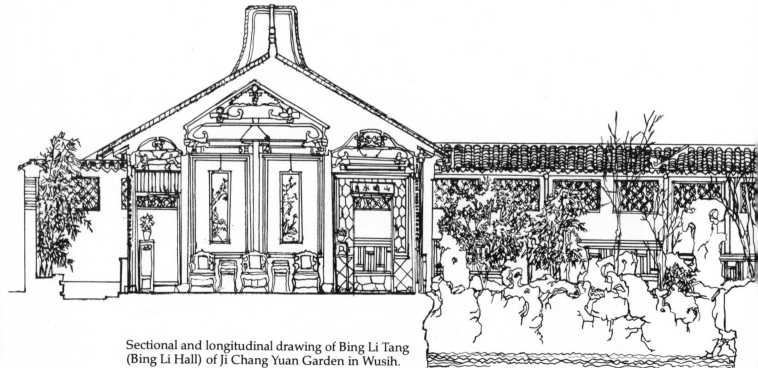

Sectional and longitudinal drawing of Bing Li Tang (Bing Li Hall) of Ji Chang Yuan Garden in Wusih.

This garden was designed to illustrate the construction of a garden in terms of local typographical conditions and the surrounding environment. If created today it might be viewed as a demonstration garden to elucidate the concept of designing with Nature. As the garden site slopes down gradually from west to east along the foot of the mountain, the rockeries were built on the highest southwest point while the ponds, which were the focal point of the composition, were excavated in the lower east side. Though the water surfaces were not large, they were clear as mirrors. The design of this garden, though built in limited space, effectively enlarged the field of vision by borrowing scenery from the Wei Shan Mountain. The ingenious placement of pavilions, terraces, and bridges at unique scenic spots as well as the landscape use of rockeries, ponds, fountains, creeks and plants suitable to local conditions make this small garden one of the best in China.

General plane figure of Bing Li Tang (Ceremony Hall) Courtyard of Ji Chang Yuan Garden of Wusih.

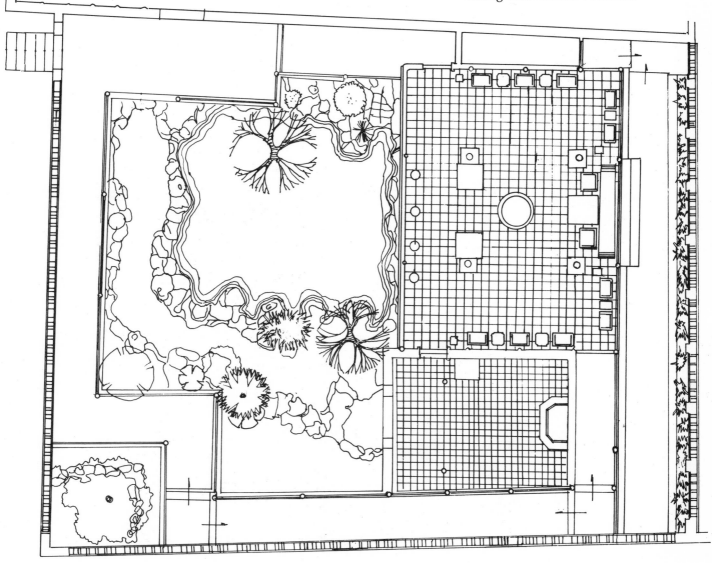

THE JIN SHAN MOUNTAIN OF ZHEN JIANG

Jin Shan Mountain is located in the north-west of Zhen Jiang City in Jiangsu Province on the south bank of the Yangtse River. It is famous not only for grand mountain scenery but also for the mists which rise from the waves which stretch far up and down the river. In the middle of the 4th century under the Southern Chin Dynasty, a large temple garden, the Jin Shan Si, was built from the foot to the top of the Jin Shan Mountain. It consisted of a number of halls, courtyards, pavilions, terraces, and a pagoda the Ci Shou Ta. The latter was a 7-storied structure constructed of wood with balustrades and passageways on every story for viewing scenes from all sides — the vast Yangtse River to the north, the city built on hilly land to the south, and the old Yangchow city indistinctly seen in cloud and mist on the opposite side of the river. The mist is created by waves lashing the rocks at the foot of the mountain, sending up a pearly spray. The Jin Shan Mountain, covered by the architectural splendour of the temple blended with the beauty of surrounding landscapes, makes it one of the best of the well-known scenic areas in China.

Bird's-eye view of West Lake in Hangchow.

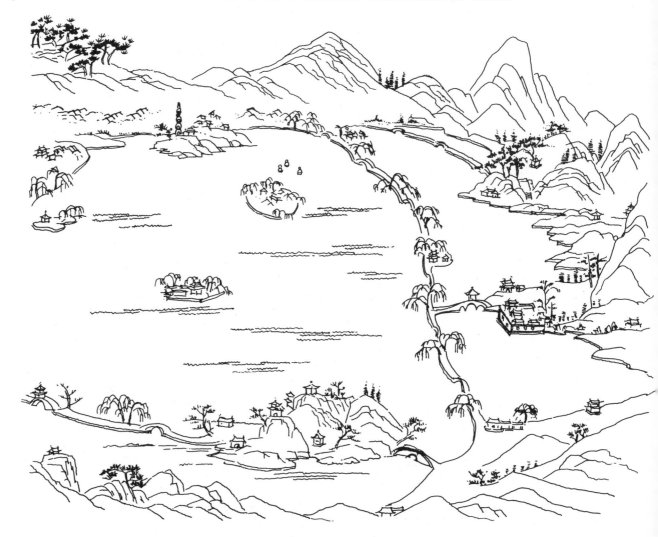

188 *The Garden Art of China*

Hangchow was one of the six ancient capitals of China. Early in the 13th century an Italian traveler, Marco Polo, who traveled to and stayed for years in China, praised Hangchow as one of the most beautiful and graceful cities in the world. The placid West Lake was

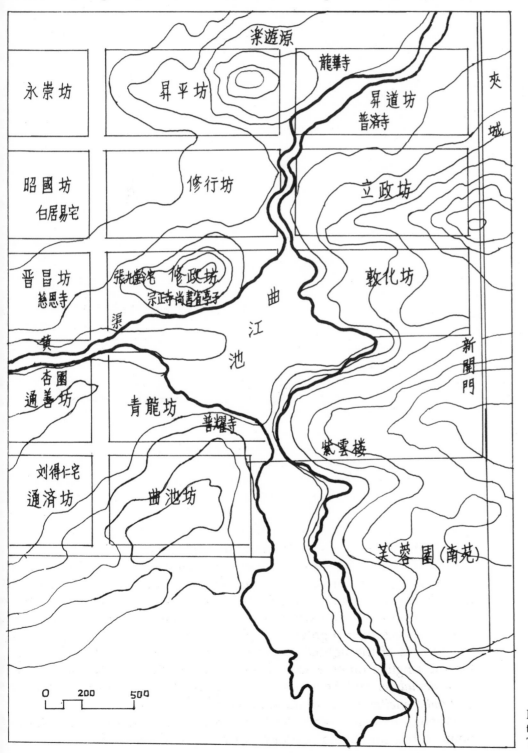

Plane figure of Qu Jiang flowing through Chang An, the Capital of Tang Dynasty (7–10th Century).

Practical Patterns of Chinese Gardens 189

曲院風荷

Qu Yuan Feng He (Bend Courtyard Lotus Features) during the time of Yong Zheng of the Qing Dynasty, beginning of 18th Century. This was one of the ten scenes of West Lake.

the center of the splendid landscape presented by the city. Its water surface measures about six square kilometers. It is surrounded by gorgeous mountains covered with green forests and dotted with clear springs. In short, its topographical situation presents a unique combination of plains and hilly land graced with rich water resource from rivers and creeks. This rich natural setting led to Hangchow being styled "the ten best scenic spots in the world".

One of them, the San Tan Yin Yue (Three Ponds Reflecting the Moon) is a green forested islet formed into a lagoon — "an islet in the big lake and a small lake in the islet". The small lake was embellished with three small white pagodas of stone built at the water surface. Candles were lighted at night in the apertures of the pagodas. The images of the lighted pagodas reflect in water like the full moon. On the ringlike outer embankment *Rosa hybrida, Syringa oblata, Magnolia denudata,* and begonias were planted. Lotus, Chinese water-lily (*Nelumbo nucifera*), was planted in the nearby waters.

Through its many years West Lake has developed a host of associations with a number of Chinese leading poets, artists and gardeners.

The poetic flavour and picturesque beauty of the spot drew them to it and they in turn added to its luster in their depictions of it. One of the most famous was the poet Su Dong Po of the Northern Song Dynasty. For some years he was the magistrate of Hangchow and built an embankment at West Lake. It was later named Su Di (Su Embankment) to memorialize not only the man and his poetry but his contribution to West Lake as well.

Along the lakeside, pavilions, halls and rockeries are faintly visible among the green trees which clothe the islands. Among the more notable scenes on the lake are the pavilion Hu Xin Ting (Pavilion in Mid-lake) and a mounded islet Ruan Gong Dun (Master Ruan's Mound) placed as foils not only for each other but to the water kiosk Hua Gong Guan Yu (Viewing Fish at Hua Gong Pond), Huang Lung Tung (the Rockeries of Yellow Dragon Cave), Ku Shan (the Autumn Woods on Solitary Hill), and Tao Shih Ta (the Pleasure Stone Pagoda).

THE CHENGTEH IMPERIAL MOUNTAIN RESORT OF JEHOL PROVINCE

The Chengteh Imperial Resort, built between 1702 and 1792, is an architectural treasure, with beautifully landscaped gardens. Historically, it was called the Jehol Provisional Palace.

The Chengteh Imperial Mountain Resort encompassed an area of 600 ha. (1,384 acres) surrounded by a 10 kilometer-long stone wall. Built into the wall at various points were eight Outer Monasteries. This resort was started during the reign of Emperor Kangxi and completed by Emperor Qianlong, the grandson of Kangxi. The resort was divided into two parts: the palace region and the landscape garden region which in turn was divided into three distinct garden areas; the mountain garden, the lake garden and the plain ground garden. Each garden had its unique features and while conceived as independent, they were designed to relate in a unified system.

The lake area was manually excavated, reforming the original topographical features to imitate the Tai Hu Lake of Wusih and West Lake of Hangchow. The method of landscaping the lake was also similar to that of the gardens in the lower reaches of Yangtse River, namely, to lay out islets in the lake and to landscape the surroundings.

The lake was separated into several sections by emplacing embankments or hills. The water surface in northeast is the largest and widest. The lesser water surfaces are not only narrower and longer but also built in zigzag configurations to extend the viewer's sense of their extent. The lake was designed not only for its intrinsic beauty but to reflect the landscape built along its banks. The shapes of the islets are greatly varied, some of them are connected to banks by embankments and bridges to create beautiful waterscapes, while others were formed like peninsulas projecting into the water.

Reproduced drawing of Qi Xiu Tang (Beautifully-setting Hall) of Chengteh Summer Resort.

The mountain garden was constructed to imitate natural mountains. Aged pines and cypresses were preserved and others were added. Magnificent halls and pavilions were built up the mountain ascending from the lake area or in the valleys interspersed between the mountains. This garden possesses all the exquisiteness of a mountain resort, in a simply unique and splendid fashion.

The imperial palace was located in the plain area. It was built with the square courtyard characteristic of North China. The several landscapes surrounding it were faithful copies of famous gardens of central China. The architectural styles of the buildings followed those associated with the Han, Mongolian and Tibetan.

Practical Patterns of Chinese Gardens   193

General plane figure of Chengteh Mountain Resort: 1. court   2. Ru Yi Zhou (Good Luck Islet)   3. Cheng Hu (Clear Lake)   4. Jing Hu (Mirror Lake)   5. Ru Yi Hu (Good Luck Lake)   6. Yan Yu Lou (Misty Rain Storey)   7. Jin Shan (Gold Hill)   8. Shui Xin Xie (Central Water-pavilion)   9. Wen Yuan Shi Zi Lin (Wen Yuan Lion Grove)   10. Mo Shu Yuan (Ten Thousand Trees Arboretum)   11. Re He Quan (Jehol Well)   12. Song Yun Xia (Cloudy-pines Gorge)   13. Li Shu Xia (Pear-trees Gorge)   14. Song Lin Xia (Pine Forest Gorge)   15–22. the Eight Outer Monasteries.

The scenic spots of Jin Shan (Golden Mountain) in Zhen Jiang.

Practical Patterns of Chinese Gardens   195

THE LEADING NATURAL LANDSCAPES OF CHINA

To help the reader better understand the Chinese passion for beautiful landscapes and the conventions and principles employed by Chinese landscape artists in creating gardens, a brief account of some of the most highly prized natural landscapes in China may be useful. As the attentive reader will have noted, we have described several natural areas highly prized in the Chinese esthetic tradition but which were modified and enhanced in keeping with Chinese landscaping principles. The scenes described in this section are keystones found in the natural landscape against which the Chinese artists have compared and judged the value of man-made landscapes over the centuries.

As will be apparent the significant elements found by poets, philosophers and artists in these natural landscapes are not only esthetic but metaphysical and ethical. The best of Chinese thought and culture has always seen human life and conduct embedded in a larger natural order. As a consequence, the Chinese view of the world encompasses at all times a profound sense of how the world operates and is organized (metaphysics and cosmology), how mankind should behave (ethics) and what is beautiful (esthetics). All of these considerations are interrelated and bind together in the response of the cultured person to natural landscapers. In an analogous way they are interrelated and employed in creating the high art of gardening.

The reader is urged while reading the following descriptions to recall this interrelatedness of what the Chinese consider fundamentally valuable as they read this book.

The Yellow Mountains

The range of Yellow Mountains in Anhwei Province is famous for its aged pines, thousands of years old situated on its high cliffs; the wonderful upright huge rocks which punctuate every view; the "Sea of Clouds" under the peaks; and the hot springs in the mountain valleys. They are popularly named the Si Jui (Four Absolutes).

The cliffs are styled "the most wonderful cliffs in China". There are seventy-two peaks in the Yellow Mountains, of which the highest is called Tian Du Feng (The Peak of Heaven) at an altitude of 1,800 m.

The "Sea of Cloud" is a wonder. Before sunrise or on misty days the clouds float layer upon layer in varied shapes and groups under the peaks making them look like islets in the vast sea. At sunrise, the clouds take on marvelous colours which only the insensitive do not find compellingly beautiful.

The waterscapes of the Yellow Mountain Valley are picturesque and entrancing. They include two lakes, sixteen springs and fountains, twenty-four creeks and many ponds and pools. The most famous is the waterfall Jiu Long Pu (Nine Dragon Waterfalls). The water falls over the projecting cliffs of Xianglu Feng (Incense Burner Cliffs) just like nine dragons flying straight down out of sight.

The Yellow Mountains are one of the outstanding landscapes in China for their beautiful form and waterscapes.

Scene of Yellow Mountains (Huangshan Mountains) of Anhwei Province.

The Tai Hu Lake of Wusih

Tai Hu is one of the five great fresh-water lakes in China. Its boundless expanse of blue water (about 2,400 sq. km) extends into two provinces, Kiangsu and Chekiang. Wusih borders the north side of the lake and is the most beautiful area of landscapes. It includes a 300 sq. km water surface with a number of large and small islets. It is just like a scroll of mountains and waters surrounded by hilly land with attractive peninsulas, bays, forests and a vast area of green vegetation along the lakeside.

The lake side has been enhanced by the following outstanding gardens:

Mei Yuan (The Plum Garden) was established at the end of Qing Dynasty in 1912. This garden is planted with thousands of plum trees and features beautiful pavilions, halls, terraces and a pagoda on a commanding elevation. From the third story of the pagoda, the beautiful landscapes of Tai Hu Lake can all be seen.

Winter scene of Lushan Mountain, Kiangsi.

Summer scene of Shiangshan (Fragrance) Hill, Beijing.

A corner of the
famous East
Lake of
Shaoxing.

Yuan Tou Zhi (The Head of Soft-shelled Turtle) is a scenic spot, where the natural landscape of Tai Hu is beautified by traditional Chinese garden architecture. In the lake there are three small hilly islets called San Shan (Three Mountains) at an elevation of 50 m for viewing the surrounding waterscapes in Tai Hu Lake.

Li Yuan was a private garden of three parts: a group of rockeries, a long corridor in the east of about 300 m connected to a pavilion in the lake and a long embankment along the lake side with a pavilion projecting into the lake. On the wall of the corridor there are 89 apertures of different floral patterns and inlaid with carved stones written by calligraphers Su Dong Pu and Huang Yang Min.

A waterscape of Tai Hu Lake of Wusih, the Dongtingshan Mountains seen on the opposite side.

THE LANDSCAPE OF KWEILIN IN KWANGSI

Kweilin is a beautiful city on the Li Jiang River of Kwangsi province. It is famous for its wonderful caverns and the ribbon-like blue water winding through hilly banks.

Fu Bo Shan (Emerald-like Mountain Above Blue Wave) arises on the bank of the Li Jiang River and projects into the river. Numerous pavilions have been built from the mountain foot up the mountain for the visitors to rest and view the waterscapes of the Li Jiang River. Their reflected images from the blue water are marvelously fascinating.

Xian Bi Shan (Elephant-nose Mountain) presents the appearance of an elephant sucking water from the river, so its name.

Chuan Shan (Piecing-through Mountain) is another mountain beside the Li Jiang River. There is a large hole near the peak through which visitors can look from south to north. It is a curious and wonderful feature.

In addition to these three scenic spots we should mention some of the well-known natural scenic regions — mountains, rivers and lakes — of China.

The Five Mountains of China

Mount Taishan (East Mountain), one of the Five Mountains of China. In ancient times it was known as Daishan. It towers over the vast plain of Taian in Shantung Province. The poet Du Fu of the Tang Dynasty said of it, "From the top you see all the other peaks prostrating themselves below."

Visitors usually follow the stone steps of the central route up the slope and descend by the western route. Beautiful scenes meet the eye at every turn and cultural relics dot the trail. Daiding is the highest point in the Taishan Range. The most noteworthy scenes are the South Heavenly Gate, the Jade Emperor's Crown, the Zhanlu Terrace, the Emerald Cloud Temple, and the Fairy Bridge.

Mount Hengshan of Hunan Province.

Above, Hengshan Mountain; *Left,* Northern Mountain of Hengshan Mountain; *Right,* Wu Gorge of the Yangtse River, famous for its twists and turns.

Snow on Huashan Mountain.

West peak of
Huashan
Mountain.

Mount Hengshan, popularly known as the South Mountain, lies in Hengshan County, Hunan Province. It is the lowest of the Five Mountains. It has 72 peaks, of which Zhurong, the main peak, is over 1,200 m above sea level. The mountain arises near the Xiangjiang River and its peaks are always hidden in mist and clouds.

Mount Huashan (the West Mountain) and the third of the Five Mountains, rises majestically above Weihe River Plain in Huayin County, Shensi Province. With its steep cliffs sightseers must be of stout heart and prepared to use a variety of means to reach its 1,997 m peak. First, they must use iron chain ladders on ninety degree cliffs, then climb the "1,000-Foot-Long Flight of Stone Steps", and finally pass through a narrow rocky defile which permits only one person to pass at a time. The mountain has five peaks — the East, South, West, North and Central — all connected by breath-taking passages and plank paths clinging to the cliffs.

Emei Mountain is another of the famous Five Buddhist Mountains. It is located in Szechwan Province. The Tang poet Li Bai (701 — 762)

Emei Mountain of Szechwan Province.

said of Emei that it is "loftier than the Western Heaven". A 60 km staired path leads from the foot to the summit. Along the way monasteries hide behind trees, springs gurgle, monkeys call, and birds sing in the forest. The most famous monasteries situated on the mountain are Serve the Country, Noise of Thunder, Ten-Thousand-Years and Huacang.

Mount Jiuhua is the last of the famous Five Buddhist Mountains. It rises in Qingyang County, Anhwei Province. It was named Mount Lingyang in the Han Dynasty (206 B.C. — A.D. 220) but was renamed Jiuhua (Nine Flowers) from two lines of the poet Li Bai: "Seen from afar, Nine-Flower-Peak is more graceful than nine lotus flowers". The mountain is the site of a great number of temples and monasteries. Between the Ming and Qing Dynasties (14th to 20th centuries) as many as 300 monasteries were built on its slopes.

Mount Jiuhua in Anhwei Province.

The Yangtse River

The Three Gorges of the Yangtse River — Wu Gorge, Xiling Gorge and Qutang Gorge — are well-known for their majestic and awe-inspiring features.

Wu Gorge, runs for 40 km through the Wushan Mountain Range. It is famous for its convoluted twists and turns. Fairy Peak is the most majestic of the 12 peaks along its banks.

Xiling Gorge, 156 km in length, is the longest of the Three Gorges. Fascinating, tranquil scenes closely follow one another along both banks.

Qutang Gorge is 8 km long but flanked by precipitous cliffs. The narrowest passage in the Gorge is only 100 m wide. The stream at this point is so rapid that only skilled boatmen can safely navigate it. But so marvelous are the high cliffs and the rapids that not only the Chinese but foreign tourists make the trip despite its hazards.

The Famous Lakes of China

Some of the natural lakes of China are marked by unique features which draw both the Chinese and others to marvel at their wonders.

Qinghai Lake in Qinghai Province is famous for the Bird Isle in the western part of the lake. It measures less than 0.1 sq. km but is a paradise of 100,000 birds — bar-headed geese, brown-headed gulls, fish gulls and cormorants. It is one of the most remarkable and compelling sights in the world. It is a natural preserve now strictly controlled by the government.

Lake Dongting and the Yueyang Tower. The Tower stands in western Yueyang County, Hunan Province, on the bank of Lake Dongting. The three-storied structure built in the Tang Dynasty (618 — 907) became known only after Fan Zhongyan (989 — 1052), a noted man of letters of the Northern Song Dynasty, wrote the article *Notes of the Yueyang Tower* in its praise. The Tower commands a magnificent view of the vast lake which joins the mountains and the Yangtse River in the distance.

Dian Chi Lake, a beautiful alpine lake 1,800 m above sea level with an area of 330 sq. km on the southern outskirts of Kunming, Yunnan Province. West Mountain bordering one shore is also known as the Mountain of the Sleeping Beauty.

Peacock Lake is in Xishuangbana Dai Autonomous Prefecture, Yunnan Province. In this hot and damp climate are found such rare and wonderful animals and birds as peacocks, hornbills, elephants and rhinoceroses.

Index